ANGELS AND FAIRIES IN NAGALAND

Lt Col. S.S. Pandit (Late)

INDIA • SINGAPORE • MALAYSIA

ISBN
Hardcase 979-8-89632-481-2
Paperback 979-8-89556-339-7

This book is not a work of fiction. References to real people, events, establishments, organizations, or locales are true.

In the midst of humiliation and so-called defeat and tempestuous life I am able to retain my peace because of an underlying faith in God translated as truth.

– Mahatma Gandhi

Dedicated to the memory of late Shri Markus Angami, late Shri Satsuo Angami, late Sri Surendra Mohan Kumar, late Shri K. Mehta, and a score of my friends in Naga Hills who sacrificed their lives for the nation and for the good of our people.

– S.S. Pandit

CONTENTS

PREFACE

Naga Hills is inhabited by simple, innocent, intelligent, and proud people. They have their own culture, faith, codes of morals, and sorrows and are rich in love. They also live in a well-knit democratic society.

My association with the Nagas began as early as 1951. Since then, I have acquired a liking for them and formed a circle of close friends! During my four-year stay in Naga Hills, my official tenure of duty, I strived to serve them and our nation! I shared their joy and sorrow and the moments of highest excitement with them.

Their people who became my friends trusted me, and fortunately, even the hostiles developed faith in me! This turned out to be a challenge as they expected me to solve their difficulties of diverse types, fulfill the role of a mentor, bless them, and give advice. This gave me enough confidence to deal with delicate issues and domestic matters.

As I narrate my experiences in my book: the exciting ones, Nagas' reactions to the shortcomings of others, especially of the administrators, their thoughts on inhabitants of adjoining hilly areas, and others on various important subjects concerning the people of the region, I had to take recourse to add a few tidbits as asides!

Providentially, my association with residents of tribal areas began at a very young age when I accompanied my father to the regions of the central provinces. There, my grandfather was one of the few Indians to become a deputy commissioner (collector) in the central provinces and serve as the Dewan in the princely states.

I took a great liking for these residents as they looked after me, especially the family driver who hailed from the tribal areas. Later, my command of Gurkha and Garhwali troops increased my affection for them (tribals). Not only did I come in close contact with them while serving in Assam, but I also had the chance to live with them and adopt their philosophy, thus enabling me to develop my style. Also, to serve and love them with the aim of service to the nation.

I was born in Nagpur, which was the capital of the Central Provinces, renamed Madhya Pradesh after independence. The reorganization mapped it into Bombay State, and then the bifurcation of the state brought it under the cover of Maharashtra. Like my birthplace, I have also more or less lost my individuality as a Maharashtrian or Nagpurian while serving in the army and the government services within India and outside.

Due to this fundamental psychological change, I have learned to consider myself as one belonging to the people of the place where I live and work. The roots of my cosmopolitan life and beliefs lie deep in the way my parents brought us up. Caste, creed, provincialism, and communalism were not part of our life as far as my memory goes. My father's best friends hailed from the United Kingdom, Hyderabad, Coorg, Gujarat, and Punjab.

I am grateful to Sarvashri Vitaulie Angami and Tatsan Nagli for their assistance. I acknowledge with delight and pride the help and encouragement from my daughter Kshiteeja. Without her support, I wouldn't have completed the book.

In the end, I appeal to all not to misinterpret or misunderstand what is written. It is without malice toward any individual or organization. The incidents and experiences have been narrated with the hope that the reader understands the spirit and depth of the words used in the book and will guide them toward what is right. It perhaps may prove to be of some benefit spiritually, materially, and morally.

INTRODUCTION OF "ANGELS AND FAIRIES IN NAGALAND" – VIJAY PARANJAPE

This anthology of 40 short stories entitled Angels and Fairies in Nagaland was written well over 60 years ago. Why the manuscript remained shrouded in obscurity for so long has been briefly explained by the author's daughter, Ms. Bhagyashree Ranade, in her foreword to the book.

At first glance, the stories and the text may appear to be outdated, but as one reads further, one quickly notices the similarities between the events and circumstances in the 1950s and the tragic events that took place in mid-2023, especially in the state of Manipur. The actors have changed, but the consequences are just as painful.

Lt. Col. S.S. Pandit's stories bring home the fact that human nature remains fundamentally the same even though the events described and the locations where they occur may be decades and hundreds of miles apart. The merit of his writings lies in the fact that the style is rather simple but very communicative. It is very much like the way the tribal folks think and talk. But at times, when the author expresses his thoughts, the language becomes more complex and contemplative. The stories are all based on facts and narrated in a lucid style. They are about incidents that took place, people who lived, and many who left a mark on history. To name just a few, there are famous and well-known people like General Thimayya, Lt. Gen. S.S.P. Thorat, S.M. Dutt (I.P), and Fazal Ali, the then Governor of Assam. Also, he refers to Angami Zapu Phizo, who had fought for decades to achieve independence for the Naga people, and his old and ailing mother who insisted on meeting Lt. Col. S.S. Pandit since she has full faith in him and believed that he alone could understand her thoughts and last wish. Such poignant moments apart, there are simple young men, fair maidens, fierce warriors, and pacifist Gandhians like Natwarbhai Thakkar, who ran the only ashram in the region, ceaselessly advocating for negotiation and reconciliation between the local communities and the establishment.

Generally speaking, people expect officers of the Indian Armed Forces and the Intelligence Bureau to be hard-hearted and tough individuals, almost incapable of appreciating or expressing the nuances and subtleties of (softer) emotions of unsophisticated and naïve tribals. The author weaves together simple shades of emotions into meaningful and interesting short stories. Each episode expresses jealousies and envy, pleasures and pain, and inevitably the fears and dangers experienced by common folk whose lives and land are continuously infested with both armed insurgents (or freedom fighters depending on the point of view) on one side and soldiers of military and paramilitary forces on the other. What struck me was the author's ability to use his wit and presence of mind while solving problems of a personal nature, or those which involved arbitration between large groups of stubborn and belligerent people.

When I went through the book a second time, I felt that for a reader in 2024, the stories provide no historical or socio-political context in which the stories could be appreciated. Sixty years is a long span in history. In the following section, therefore, an attempt has been made to give some history of the North East Region before Independence— and some landmark events which demonstrate that the Manipur violence and tragic events that followed thereafter were not sudden or spontaneous but were a result of a series of protests which were at best either misunderstood by the establishment and neglected over the last 7 decades. But before we come to such vexatious problems, let us quickly look at the history because it is unfortunate that people of "mainstream India," both young and old, know very little about the history and socio-political priorities of the people of the Northeast.

During ancient times, especially during the epochal period of the Ramayana and the Mahabharata, the Northeastern region was called "Kamarupa" where Shiva's wife Parvati was said to have sacrificed her life due to the discourtesy shown by her father to Shiva. The Kamakhya temple stands at Gauhati as a testimony to this event. Much later in 1228 AD, Sukhapaa – a Chinese Prince of Mong – Mao (Yunar Province today) controlled the region broadly covering Myanmar in the south and southern China in the North saddled over the current Northeastern States in India – in the middle. The region was called 'Ahom Kingdom'. Thus from 1228 to 1826 – for a continuous period of 6 hundred years, the Kingdom remained a sovereign country. Tribal Groups from Burma, Nepal, China, and Tibet, each with its diverse ethnicities, migrated to the mountainous hilly areas and to the lower valleys of Dibang, Dihang, Lohit, and many others which formed tributaries in the low Brahmaputra River basin. But despite the diversity in languages, culture, cuisine, and ethnicities, the people of the Northeast have developed an identity of their own.

During the British period, the region was annexed via the "Treaty of Yangdaboo" in 1826, and their rule extended over the Jaintia Hill and Cachar, with Shillong as the capital of Assam (a corrupted version of Ahom). After Independence, Khatris and Chuttrias settled in these hills, and large-scale migration of Bengalis from Bangladesh and West Bengal has been witnessed. It is therefore no surprise that the Northeastern people, hill tribes, feel that their identity is at stake.

The root of unrest among the Naga and other tribes in the North East can be understood partly by learning about Angami Zapu Phizo, who was a nationalist leader of the Naga tribes, and partly by recognizing the role played by the American Missionaries who played an important evangelical role in the conversion of almost half of the population of Nagaland, Southern Arunachal, Assam, and Manipur – from their ancient religious practices to Christianity. The third element was the invocation and imposition of the Armed Forces Special Power Act (AFSPA -1958) in practically the whole of the Northeast (excluding Tripura, Assam, and Meghalaya). These 3 elements and the inability or the lack of conscious perception of the situation by the Central Indian establishment were primarily responsible for the near intractable mess that the Northeast faces. The rest of India had so many of their problems to grapple with that they had no time to tackle the Northeast.

Angami Zapu Phizo established the Naga Nationalist Council (NNC), which asserted that Naga tribes were never under any foreign rule — British, Indian, or any other administration — and therefore had the right to self-determination. His so-called freedom movement took the form of armed resistance after 1958 when the AFSPA was imposed by the Government. In the early 1946-47, as the British were preparing for their final withdrawal from India, A. Z. Phizo separately met the Assamese, Garos, Khasis, Lushais, Mishmis, and Meiteis, and other leaders in the Northeast to form independent countries of their own. Consequently, A. Z. Phizo was in Calcutta Presidency Jail in 1948, but in 1949, he again joined the Naga National Council (NNC) and was elected its President. His efforts at secession continued, and in 1994, he formed the "People's Sovereign Republic of Nagaland" with the help of Chang Chiefs of Tuensang. This made the Delhi Government, especially Jawaharlal Nehru, very unhappy, and to curb such secessionist tendencies, he invoked the AFSP Act in 1958, which completely changed the situation.

The Assam Police and the paramilitary battalion were deployed with other central forces. The village of Mokakchung had meticulously kept a diary of all the acts of loot, rape, and torture of local people that took place between 1954 and 1964, i.e. precisely at the time when Lt. Col. S.S. Pandit was stationed in the Nagaland Hills as an Officer of the Intelligence Bureau.

But there was a strong ray of hope for the militant secessionists and the Armed Forces of the Government of India. It was the Gandhi ashram in Chuchuyimlang, the only institute that was non-official and non-Christian Missionary in Nagaland. It was run by Natwarbhai Thakkar - a rare & dedicated Gandhian who believed that following truth is the highest form of worship and non-violent actions based on it were service to God. Accordingly, the institute, against all odds, gave vocational training, especially on weaving on looms, on health and hygiene, and achieving peace and amity through negotiation and reconciliation. In this context, Gen. S.S.P. Thorat had paid a visit to the ashram and after hearing about the work being done, he is said to have remarked, "If we only had half a dozen Natwarbhais, Nagaland would not need the army."

The title Angels and Fairies in Nagaland may sound a bit strange to readers, but to clarify the puzzle, the author himself reveals the meaning. In one of the stories, he quotes the local people who quipped, "Angels have arrived, let us hope that they bring peace and prosperity." In common parlance, the locals had nicknamed all newly posted young officers angels, and the young youth remarked, "Whether we get peace or not, one thing is sure; that the news of the young officers will delight the fairies in our land." Readers may note that the Naga Society is matriarchal, brides don't pay dowries, and widows have the freedom to remarry or lead their lives according to their wishes.

On the 1st of December 1963, Nagaland was granted statehood and became the 16th state of India, and conditions were expected to improve. Unfortunately, they did not, and violence and disturbances continued. In 1975, the Naga Peace Council signed the Shillong Peace Accord, wherein Nagaland gave up its demand for a special nationhood and accepted the supremacy of the Indian Constitution. A large number of militants surrendered their weapons.

The current relevance of the book becomes clear when we compare the stories of the 1950s with the events that occurred in 2023. The simmering anger and the huge trust deficit during the last decade or so came to a head when the Citizens Amendment Bill was passed in 2016. The people of the Northeast felt that their states would again be swamped by Hindu Bangladeshis in addition to earlier migrants. This feeling was strengthened when thousands of teachers and students protested the Citizen Amendment Act, which was passed in 2020, and there was unrest in Dimapur. Moreover, the further extension of AFSPA was approved by the GOI. In mid-2023, when the State Govt of Manipur, dominated by Meiteis , violently clashed with the Kukis in hill areas. The immediate spark that lit the fire was the Manipur High Court's Order, which asked the State Government to recommend to Delhi that the dominant Meiteis should be granted "Scheduled Tribe" status, implying that the Government administration would be drafting in more Meiteis, which the Kukis in the adjoining hilly areas fear the most. This meant that the army would continue to perform civilian security duties.

The socio-cultural, economic, and administration from the book by Lt Col Pandit reflect the character of the author himself. Firstly, he believed in being upright and professional both as a soldier and as an agent of the Intelligence Bureau, and his life was based on his fundamental belief that truth, however unpalatable it may be, must be told, which he did through his official dispatches to the Government. Secondly, he was acutely aware of the complete faith the local communities had in him – and this was reciprocated by all the advice he gave them and actions he performed within his jurisdiction. It was a balancing act he performed with wit and alacrity, and simultaneously he remained loyal to his master and affectionate to his people. And lastly, the stories cleverly hid his inner anger and frustration which he felt rather strongly – because the government paid no heed to his advice regarding the need to open and sustain an honest dialogue with the tribal community until the discussions and negotiations could yield reconciliation and amity without the use of force and oppression.

Lastly, if he were alive, he would have strongly advised the government in Delhi and the States to carry forward the conclusions reached in the Shillong Peace Accord of 1975, wherein the tribals had agreed to accept the supremacy of the Indian constitution and the so-called "hostiles" had willingly surrendered their arms in the interest of peace and prosperity. Sadly, successive Central and State Governments during the last 50 years were unable to find a solution for the recent tragic situation. One hopes that Col. Pandit's book persuades the Indian government and society alike to see the truth and bring about the necessary course correction.

ABOUT THE BOOK

By Lt. Gen. Raghunath. PVSM, AVSM, PHS (Retd), MD, DCP, FRCPath, FAMS

Thank you for sending me the book 'Angels and Fairies' by Lt. Col SS Pandit.

I have gone through the book and found it interesting.

Col. Pandit summarizes the work in his preface well. He has recorded his experiences during his four-year tenure in the Naga Hills-Tuensang Agency, as the area was known then.

The basic characteristics of the Nagas are quite like those of tribal groups in the rest of the country. These people have a simplistic ethos that guides their societies. The lack of 'societal' skills, deception, and manipulation of interactions make them vulnerable to exploitation. This was true of the Nagas at the time covered by the work. Since then, political changes have surely changed them, at least in the urban areas.

The Naga population is divided into different tribes which have their customs and languages. The dialects differed considerably. The tribal pride resulted in conflicts leading to head-hunting. The advent of Christianity largely curbed these practices. The insularity was somewhat enhanced by the 'benign neglect' of the colonial masters of the Indian subcontinent. They isolated the Nagas, leaving them to continue with their tribal organization. However, they provided access to Christian missionaries. This has resulted in the adoption of religion by a large proportion of the population. It has been pointed out in the book that not all Nagas have given up their former animalistic beliefs.

This has been a mixed blessing, while the inter-tribal violence has curbed political integration into the body politic of India, has been hampered.

The desire to carve out an independent nation arose along with Indian independence. This was spearheaded by A.Z. Phizo. His role has been dealt with in parts of the book. It is clear that the entire population of Naga Hills was not militant, but their terror was a looming threat throughout. While it has not died out, the political changes have diminished the impact. Statehood has changed the scenario. Nevertheless, the Naga problem still exists and raises its head from time to time.

I have noted down some interesting episodes recounted in the book but would not repeat them here. Two instances are noteworthy, one of the responses to the posting of Sikh troops in the area and another one of demand for compensation for a missing dog! There is still an apprehension among those posted in the area for their pets lest they turn up in the Kohima market.

Overall, the book made interesting reading of the experiences of a successful political agent. The final pages of the author's prescriptions for the administration of a difficult area are probably somewhat outdated since they end in the late 1950s. With this reservation, I would recommend the book as a good read.

ACKNOWLEDGMENT

The book Angels and Fairies in Nagaland was written by my late father, Lt. Col. S.S. Pandit, in the 1960s after his tenure in Kohima, Nagaland.

It has been a long, long time ago, and we, his children, take great pride in publishing his book, which gives great insight into Nagaland. He would have been mighty pleased to see this book on the stands, being read by young and old.

Some helped bring this book to fruition, and I am grateful to all of them. Once this book started to go ahead, from a typewritten manuscript on paper that was fragile to a computerized version, many people were involved who deserved to be acknowledged and thanked.

I take this opportunity to thank Vijay Paranjape, Lieutenant General Deepak Summanwar, Lt. Gen. Raghunath, Uday Vaidya, Major General S. Pitre, and others. Thanks to Doreswamy Srinidhi for reading, content editing, and rearranging the chapters with appropriate titles! This encouraged me to publish the book written by my (Late) father, for it has some timeless values to teach.

I would like to thank the publishers, Notion Press Media Pvt Ltd, for their support.

FOREWORD: BHAGYASHREE REMEMBERS

My father's book on a subject of immense national interest literally arrived at my home when our ancestral home was sold, to my great surprise and astonishment, even though he wrote this book in the 1960s. I knew of the existence of the manuscript; however, I had not been able to lay my hands on it. When I opened the folder, I saw a typed manuscript on frail, 60-year-old paper, which was difficult to hold in case it crumpled. I now read into his character, personality, anguish, and deep thinking, and what a revelation, amazing!

At the time when the book was written, I was 7 years of age, and all I knew was that my father had some anguish. He would wake up at 4, make a hot cup of tea, sit at the dining table with our dog curled at his feet, and start typing on his typewriter, constantly holding a cigarette in his fingers. What was going on, I wondered. Each time he returned for a home visit from Kohima (Nagaland), the sad look in his weary eyes was replaced with joy on seeing the family. Yet as he sat writing, the anguish returned, and I could never fathom at that age what was happening.

Now that I have read his book, I clearly understand his angst about what was happening in Nagaland and what it was doing to him while he was in service.

I understand that our country has never really changed in many arenas, though since 2014, she has been born again on the global stage... Maybe there will be change, as we common citizens see, read, and hear today all over our nation.

Since age 7, I always wished my eyes had the memory of the past so I could remember the time spent during my holidays, which were not frequent due to Kohima being a non-family station. Yet if I try to strain my mind, I remember a few things about the route to Kohima. The winding roads going up and down the mountains, sitting in a jeep led by a convoy. And the quarters in which we lived were next to my father's office in Kohima. I have a very good memory of walking down a hillside to the cemetery where thousands of soldiers and officers were buried, and maybe many of the locals who sacrificed their lives for the nation and the good of the people.

One of the epitaphs engraved on the grave said,

"When you go home tell them of us and
say for your tomorrow
we gave our today."

This has always stayed in my memory and has never gone away because I do remember the sacrifices made by so many people as told to me by my father in the hope of peace in the region.

I am sure my siblings may have data and memories of Kohima; however, only a few were available. My father has given credit to my sister Kshiteeja for motivating him to complete the book Angels and Fairies in Nagaland.

My father was an extremely kind, affectionate, disciplined, principled, and simple person who loved us beyond anything. I can well imagine him being friendly with the people of Nagaland, whoever they were, and giving them a lot of love, affection, and kindness.

On the other side, as an army personnel and being in the intelligence field, I believe he always put together the true present situation and feelings of the people of Nagaland and tried his best to tie them to the policies that were made by the higher-ups, only to see that the Naga people get peace, a home, and survive with dignity. I also remember him trying to align the lives and requirements of the Naga people to the policies made by the central government. The endless ordeal and politics gave my father a great deal of angst, and he has had to also suffer personally in his career because of speaking the truth.

I do know now after reading the book and running through pages of letters and papers to the government leading them to see the plight of the Nagas and change their policies to meet their needs and requirements, yet it was a difficult time. I could imagine how he felt to get a negative response; nothing ever seemed to match each other. The book gives a very simplistic and beautiful picturization of the Naga people and their plight. The narration also talks about how my father tried to help them in dire circumstances, taking a risk. Perhaps this was not appreciated at that time; it is an insight of hindrances and obstacles faced aligning the government and people.

I am hoping that, though this is a different era, it will be read with interest as a historical narration of what was done for the people by the government. The book will allow an interest to be developed in the present status of Nagaland and changes, if any. Moreover, learning of how not seeing eye to eye can lead to upheaval, not only sacrifices, wins, and losses, but also people's lives and for the Nation.

The book is an extensive narration of the conditions in Nagaland, where he served for so long and so conscientiously. Thoroughly exploring all aspects — political, religious, geographical, and cultural — of this region, he has assembled a gallery of colorful portraits of the people he dealt with, resulting in a picture of one part of India few know about, including the Western world. Educational as well as inspirational, the book sheds light on the problems that beset the region.

"The incidents and experiences have been narrated in this book and if one reads the spirit and depth in the words, best of us must learn a lot from his book. It may prove to be of some benefits spiritually, materially, and morally." – Lt Col Pandit

I jot down a few of his pensive words, to evoke thoughts.

"The chain of thoughts is unending, feeling like a small pebble on the shore. Sometimes thoughts creep up at night, and I (my father) discard them saying only recently, wise men have succeeded in formulating a philosophy for Northeast Frontier Agency, based on the ideals of Prime Minister Pandit Jawaharlal Nehru. Similar work may follow for the guidance of administrators and the would-be leaders at a later stage when a definite ideology as to what is best for India and the pattern of life and society are decided upon, formulated, and finally reduced to writing."

My father, Lt. Col. S.S. Pandit, fondly referred to by us as 'Bapu', was a loving, benevolent, and trusting man, with additional attributes of being a complete workaholic, totally devoted to the upliftment of the needy and ex-servicemen. After my father's retirement, the attachment to the forces and unfulfilled dreams propelled him to start an organization called "Goodwill," Goodwill Ex-Servicemen's Co-op Society Ltd, one of the first of its kind in India.

The growth of "Goodwill" was an effort which resulted in obtaining contracts from companies and acquiring acres of land at MIDC, Bhosari, as a most important and everlasting landmark of the continuance and existence of the company today, 18 years after the demise of Lt Col Pandit. Lt Col Pandit's statue in the premises of the MIDC land, where there is parking for chassis, offices, and a workshop, is a lasting remembrance of the achievement and toil of a man who did so much for others, at times even at the cost of hardship for his own family.

Today, hundreds of ex-servicemen still retain his memory, pay their respects, and stand as examples of the vision of Col. Pandit, whose first love was not his family but the family of "GOODWILL."

Today, with the help and guidance of those officers and workers who revered my (late) father and shared his vision, "Goodwill" again stands on a threshold of prospective growth and is in its 25th year of existence. My father received a commendation (after his death).

"For distinguished service with devotion and selflessness displayed for the rehabilitation of ex-servicemen."

As one reads the Memoir of Col. S.S. Pandit's Nagaland experience, one will feel that destiny prepared him for this assignment in the Naga Hills!

1

IT WAS A DIFFERENT ROLE!

My role in Nagaland was not that of a combatant, but that of the chief of the local unit of the Intelligence Bureau, an organization of the Government of India. My job was to report on a day-to-day basis to the Central Government on the conditions prevailing in the area, as well as give appropriate and adequate intelligence of Naga hostile activities to the administration and the armed forces!

Adherence to truth was the basis of my report sent to the Central Government. The local authorities did not appreciate it; repeatedly, it made my position precarious, but I remained set in my determination to report facts despite undue pressure and threats applied against me. Nothing could deter me from reporting the truth, as I was convinced that if the policymakers at the helm were not kept correctly informed, they would lose ground despite the presence of the administrators and the armed forces.

(Admirable to say the least, and it was not easy! He was also fortunate to find support from the higher-ups in the services and the government!)

General KS Thimaiyya, the Chief of the Army Staff who came to Kohima to investigate the exactness of my reports, admitted to the Director of the Intelligence Bureau that the truth was not palatable to the then-General Officer Commanding at Kohima. He further advised that I should continue to submit reports based on the truth, and if I felt that

I could not convey any information to the General Officer Commanding, I should contact him directly.

Not long afterward, my office-cum-residence was located just opposite the war cemetery at Kohima in Naga Hills, where the famous words remind everyone of the sacrifices made by human beings to keep flying the banner of democracy and truth. It said, "When you go home, tell them of us and say: for your tomorrow, we gave our today!"

The other notable persons who came to my rescue when I was being harassed by the local authorities, and not only encouraged me to continue to report the true information, but also persuaded me to remain at the post, were the late Sir Fazal Ali, the governor of Assam, and the late Shri Govind Vallabh Pant, the then Union Home Minister. Their support strengthened my resolve!

Halfway through my service in Naga Hills, I was once again swimming through troubled waters for having adhered to the truth! However, support and encouragement from SM Dutt I.P. and Lieutenant General S P Thorat DSO enabled me to reach the shore successfully. Both heads had come on a visit to Kohima, the former as the joint director of the Intelligence Bureau and the latter as the general officer commanding in chief of the eastern command.

Shri Dutt, having raised the issue, said, "Sir, you are aware that Kohima, which is the headquarters of Naga Hills, is very well known for a famous war cemetery. When one walks through it, we come across graves of so many friends with a war reputation." General Thorat agreed with him. Shri Dutt continued, "But sir, Naga Hills and Kohima are famous for another unknown cemetery where many big and small reputations have found graves." As everyone gazed at him, he continued, "This needs no clarification."

The memory of 2 interesting lectures I heard when stationed at Jandiala Guru in Punjab is not only fresh in my memory but has an **incredibly significant influence** on my outlook and actions. At that time, I was commanding the battalion of Ghurkha rifles which had mutinied earlier against officers who commanded them. The first was a combined one by Pandit Mukul Raj Anand and Brigadier (now Major General Sarda Nand Anand) on "poetry and war" and the second lecture concerned "Yad" (remembrance). Dealing with the subject of poetry and war, both the speakers had narrated accounts from time immemorial about ambitious men who wanted to conquer the world including India. They emphasized that one shortcoming of all these invaders including the British, who ruled for 2 centuries, forced them to quit.

This shortcoming was their inability to win over the people, understand them, make them feel that the government was their own, for their benefit and good, and establish close contact with the people through their representatives. Use of sword and force was relied upon to establish and continue the rule.

Not that, at the highest level of policymaking, it was the intention to continue with the rule of sword and exploitation, but it remained so, probably due to the short-sightedness on the part of their representatives and the administrators on the spot. Not understanding the people, these administrators failed to win them over. Being engrossed in personal pleasures, ambitions, and with their superiority complex, these men not only lost the confidence of the people but also kept those at the helm in the dark about their real feelings, trends of events, and developments.

The second lecture emphasized that man, being mortal, is remembered by his actions and behavior, and hence the "Yad" (remembrance) a man leaves behind has more importance than anything else.

2

NAGAS ARE DIFFERENT

The Nagas, about 2 million, reside in Naga Hills district and the Halflong subdivision of Assam, Tuensang, and Tirap frontier divisions of the northeast frontier agency, as well as Ukhrul and Tamong Long subdivisions of Manipur state.

Nagas have many sub-groups: the Angami, Ao, Sema, Rema, Lotha, Zeliang, Sangathan, Konyak, Yinchungar, and Phom; Charg, Khenungau, and Tanghul. The sub-groups are also different in their languages, dress, customs, and traditions.

Naga Hills is a miniature India. In other states of India, there is some commonality in language, customs, and dress. However, it is very different in Assam and Naga Hills. Here in Naga Hills, every twenty miles, the dress, customs, and languages all differ, and they are all called Nagas!

All my Naga friends, old and young, literate and illiterate, with different shades of opinion, had gathered in my office, often used as a meeting room, to discuss and assess the prevalent situation!

One of the visitors abruptly changed the topic to question me, "I wonder how you have not learned any Naga language even though you have tasted 'Madhu' and 'Rohi' all these years." Unable to check my laughter, I said, "I wish that the tasting of a drink from various places could create a linguist! It would be a miracle! **If** it had been administered a few days after my birth, maybe I could have learned one of your languages, but now it appears difficult though not impossible. Anyhow, 'Madhu' and 'Rohi' all over Nagaland are the same, but you people speak fourteen different languages, and even an Ao cannot speak Angami language and vice versa. So it seems I must wait for my rebirth to master all the languages of Naga Hills and be one with each one of you here!"

'True,' one of the elderly Nagas shouted, "I have been trying to discover why only we, the Nagas, have so many different classes, with different names, customs, dress, and language. Ultimately, the other day in a dream I found the Right Answer." His friends demanded, 'Out with it! We will recommend your name for a Nobel Prize if we approve of it!'

"I will tell you," he replied. "When Adam and Eve were sent out of heaven, they landed on Earth as its first occupants. Soon they multiplied! Everyone in the fold was incredibly happy; they made friends with animals, birds, and other creatures who were already residents of the Earth. Cows provided milk to nurture their children; bullocks helped in plowing the land. Horses, camels, and elephants became familiar friends and assisted in overcoming the difficulties of communication and carrying loads. Even the pigeons volunteered to carry messages over long distances; in return, they were given food grains by the ingenious human beings. Happiness, prosperity, cooperation, and gaiety prevailed! Coexistence was practiced among human beings and wildlife in its true sense."

He continued after a pause, "One day God wanted to know the welfare of Adam and Eve and their descendants, and he sent for the director of the Heavenly Central Intelligence Bureau, who came accompanied by the joint director dealing with Earth. Not being satisfied with the report received through sources and agents, he commissioned the director and joint director to visit Earth personally and report facts with adequate proof."

He continued as all were curious and listened! "The Director and joint director returned after the first-hand study and narrated it to God, with all the proofs and a full-length documentary which was screened for 10 hours! God saw nothing but happiness, prosperity, and perfect cohesion. Not only was he amazed but taken with it. God glanced at everyone sitting around him and declared his intention to shift his abode to Earth!"

The news about his arrival on Earth caused a great stir in Hell. An emergency session of the Central Executive of the Political Bureau was called at midnight to consider whether the action of God amounted to imperialism or colonialism and to chalk out a plan of action. After prolonged discussion at a sitting which continued for 72 hours, the central executive came to the decision that the action of God amounted to the transgression of the rights of the other world and had the intentions of imperialistic design and motive of colonization; hence, there was a need for salvation and emancipation of the people. The people of Earth must be liberated.

The decision was referred to the council of action, which decided that any open hostility and conflict was inadvisable as popular support in a new place was a must. Cells were formed, followed by district and provincial committees, so that members of the central executive headed by their general secretary could conveniently infiltrate and counteract the influence of God.

The youngsters became impatient and asked what happened next. "You are already experiencing it today," he answered, and anyway I will tell you. "Soon the cells were established, and these worked to form district and prevention provincial committees. We found ourselves identified, in addition to caste, also by country! Indians, Africans, Chinese, Americans, Russians, British, etc. At the district and provincial level, we were called Nagas, Manipuri, Bengalis, Maharashtrians, Assamese, Punjabis, Khasis, Mizos and whatnot."

"The lesser devils divided the Nagas into Seemas, Aos, Angamis, Rengmas, Lothas, Zemis, Liangas, Tangkhuls, Konyaks, Chakesanga, and so many other names, and thus the devil gained an upper hand."

"But what did God do? Why did he keep silent?" The youngsters shouted, "Surely, he could have enlightened the human beings to ward off the devil?" God did everything possible to enlighten human beings, having seen that the one world of harmony, peace, and love was getting strife-stricken. He decided to set an example by taking forms of Lord Krishna, Lord Buddha, Christ, Paigambar, and Guru Nanak to guide them, and at least keep the world from disintegrating, by making them forget provincialism, linguism, and caste hatred. But alas, the devils turned it to their advantage to breach the community by creating caste hatred."

It is true that, when we enter a place of prayer or are in difficulty, we remember God and promise to behave true to his word and advice. However, the moment we stir out or are free from trouble, shadows of the devil follow us and dominate our better selves. It has not ended here, we now have so many issues dividing us, and you see that the devil turns everything upside down, but then we do not listen to the counsel of God, ignore those who are wiser and older, and those who could tell us what is good for us." He continued, "even the children indulge in anything and everything other than education, and leaving it, later to be educated in Lok Sabha, legislative assembly, in service, or take up begging on the road'.

The youngsters applauded, "You have enlightened us; we must recommend your name for a doctorate, which you have earned." God came to us for our good, but we could not tolerate happiness and prosperity and allowed Hell on this good Earth. Before they occupy our hills and lead us astray, we must educate ourselves. The old man left after shouting blessings at me and with a prayer to save the Naga Hills from the devil.

(He was an intelligent and sincere elder who had seen the way outsiders had exploited the innocence of the people of Naga Hills and wanted it changed. The story is a reflection of the changes brought into the earlier simple life of a Naga. Bombastic words and titles and a cocktail of many beliefs and influences are seen! One can see this perhaps in any village in India, which has been isolated due to its location!)

3

IT WAS A CHALLENGE TO DEAL WITH MODERN TIMES!

Nagaland is a mountainous country, with many places covered by virgin jungle and ranges of massive mountains, hills, and valleys, big and small. Before Independence, the road from Dimapur to Imphal was the only motorable passage. Since then, many important places have been connected by roads fit for vehicular traffic.

The hill peaks add glory to the landscape, reminding one of the immortal Sages guiding the destiny of mankind. Yet their isolation has made them self-centered and has molded their nature spiritually, mentally, and materially. Self-preservation, self-protection, and love for their land have made them suspicious of outsiders.

Their administrative system is simple yet sound. The village is run by a village headman called "Gaon Bura." The multiple languages have necessitated the creation of language interpreters called "Dobashis." These people, enveloped in red blankets, are a common sight in Naga Hills! Whether it is summer or winter, day or night, they wrap it around their body, especially when they are on official duty, on a visit to the town, or when attending a function. It indeed is a status symbol!

As soon as an individual is elected as a "Gaon Bura" by the village and approved by the administrator, a red blanket is given to him. The position of "Gaon Bura" is more of an honorary position. There is no fixed salary, but one-fourth of the house tax collected and deposited in the government treasury every year is given as a commission. On the other hand, the Dobashis are full-time job holders, and they get a monthly salary. Only these men are allowed to wear a red blanket, and it is considered an honor to be the recipient of a red blanket.

The Gaon Bura was a very important man in this chain of administration. He formed the village council and held meetings to discuss various measures relating to the village administration and maintenance of law and order. If there were any difficulties, he undertook a trip to the district headquarters and returned with orders from the Deputy Commissioner. During the 3 phases of cultivation, he deputed villagers to work in rotation and saw that all the government orders were conveyed through him to the village. He also provided paid labor for the government. In addition, he was responsible for the maintenance of the roads within the jurisdiction of the village and ensured the yearly subsidy from the government was utilized for the benefit of the village.

Besides, he cultivated his land for his livelihood, and it is his main source of income. One can wonder why a Gaon Bura undertakes all the additional responsibility and work for a paltry remuneration of 4 annas (25 paise) per house per year. However, the red blanket makes him the supremo of his village! In addition, he enjoys respect as an elder.

Dobashis helped Gaon Buras as interpreters for carrying out the orders of the district authorities in their respective areas. It was considered a great honor to be appointed as a personal Dobashis to the head of the administration, whom he accompanied on all tours and worked as a personal assistant, confidential secretary, and gentleman in attendance to the boss. In addition to the red blanket, Dobashis wore a red jacket, which differentiated them from the Gaon Buras. Furthermore, the majority of the Dobashis were young and stayed at the district headquarters. The area where they stayed was called the Dobashis Lines.

The head of Dobashis had both his ears cut off during encounters with other locals, yet he stuck to his post. To maintain the honor of the red blanket, many of the recipients sacrificed their lives.

Phizo and the Naga National Council made repeated efforts to persuade the elders to discard the red blankets to paralyze the government. During the peak disturbances in 1956 and 1957, a few Gaon Buras were even shot dead by the hostile Nagas; others were tortured and fined, but this institution of Gaon Buras remained loyal to the government. It was due to the affinity for and prestige of the red blanket.

So, it was but natural that many people in Naga Hills nurtured an ambition to possess a red blanket. While touring the Lotha area, as I was nearing the foothill of an important village, a 'defense' guard came forward and requested me to stop. To my surprise, an officer of my department from a nearby outpost was also there. Just then I saw some men carrying a very old man down the hill. First, I thought him to be ill and was coming down to request a lift to the hospital nearby! Then the officer clarified. A very old man, well past 80, one of the most loyal and one who had lost 2 of his sons during the disturbances, had heard that I was passing by the village and had expressed a desire to meet me.

As they neared, he tried to stand up with the help of others. Though he was too weak even to stand, he looked dignified. He greeted me as I went near him. Upset that he had taken all the trouble of coming down the hill to meet me, I told the officer and head of the village defense guard that I would have gone to his house in the village to meet him. Then I asked the old man to sit on a blanket, and I sat down by his side and offered him a cup of tea. Then I asked what I could do for him.

"Only one thing," he said slowly, "I have been loyal to the government. My 2 sons also have sacrificed their lives for the government. I have not been fortunate enough to wrap myself in the red blanket at least once before I die. I am too old and since the death of my son, I have been confined to bed. It is the first time in 6 months that I, with the help of my villagers, have come out of the house. Please honor me with a red blanket. Then I will die in peace." I promised him to do my best and try to move the administration to give him a red blanket as a reward for all that he and his family had done for the government.

On my return to Kohima, I requested the Deputy Commissioner to fulfill the wishes of the old man. He agreed. During the visit of the chief minister of Assam to Naga Hills, the old man received the gift of honor, a red blanket from the hands of the chief minister in his village. His joy knew no bounds. It so happened that before the chief minister completed his tour of Naga Hills, the old man was laid to eternal rest wrapped in the red blanket.

This red color has its domineering importance. It is the prominent color in the rainbow, and a child often likes this color best. The mighty sun displays its arrival and departure in red of different shapes. Even the bandsmen and infantrymen prefer red coats, and it is the ambition of every army officer to rise higher and higher so that he can adorn his cap with a red ribbon. Red tape, at the highest level, is dreaded more than the blows of a butcher's knife by commoners.

(Phizo: As the British were preparing for their withdrawal from India, Phizo met Assamese, Garos, Khasis, Lushais, Abors, Mishmis, and Meiteis leaders separately in an attempt to convince them to form independent countries of their own, instead of joining the proposed Union of India. However, his efforts failed. On 14 August 1947, one day before India gained its independence, Phizo declared the independence of Naga region.) Wikipedia

4

A SMALL STATE ON TOP OF HILLS

Before a Naga celebrates the marriage of his son, he builds, as required by tradition, a separate house where his son and daughter-in-law can stay independently. This custom has many advantages, the main one being that the young man begins to shoulder the responsibility of earning his livelihood and leading a life of his choice, and the daughter-in-law becomes the mistress of the house without interference from anyone.

This custom arose as a necessity and not with any intention of allowing a wedded couple to lead an independent life. The house of an average Naga consists of 3 compartments. It is often built above the ground like a Machchan used by the Shikaris. It is rectangular with a slanting low roof and decorations in front. The first compartment is a small room, which accommodates the cattle. Then there is a long, large-sized room that is used as a sitting room, kitchen, store, and bedroom. At the end, there may be a small room for storing agricultural implements or in the form of a veranda. Hence, the custom and tradition of building a separate house for a youth, on the eve of his marriage, has been due to the design and pattern of their houses, which affords privacy to one couple only.

In the center of the main room, there is a square cooking range on the ground with seating arrangements all around it. Cots, which normally are planks, are along the walls. After a day's work, the woman of the house cooks the food, and the husband and children sit around warming themselves and chatting.

Above the cooking range, meat and fish are hung in large quantities to be smoked and dehydrated for future use. Except for their weekly requirements, the rest of the food grains, which are harvested from their fields, are kept in a separate hut, a special common enclosure, away from the village!

The custom of keeping it separate and away from the village is to safeguard it against loss due to the outbreak of fire. Though kept unlocked, it is as safe as the vaults of a bank and remains intact due to moral binding on one another. This moral binding on the villages, not to commit theft of goods earned by another, by their arduous work, is indeed a virtue. When traveling, one finds huge stacks of firewood, grain, and fruits by the roadside meant for either sale or use. None but the rightful owner touches them.

Interestingly, the separation of a child from the house also begins much earlier, as soon as a boy or a girl nears the age of understanding. He or she is sent to sleep in the "Morang" so that the parents can continue to enjoy privacy, which is essential for a continuously happy life. "Morangs" are big halls, separate for girls and boys. These are built in a khel (suburb).

Grown-up children, after meals at their homes, go to sleep in the 'Morang'. It is looked after by the aged who are too old to toil for their daily bread, and their society pays them in kind or cash. Once all the inmates are collected for the night, the elderly caretakers enlighten them on the customs, traditions, and history of the Khel, families, and other important subjects before they go to bed.

This system has many advantages. A youth learns self-reliance, independence, discipline, and cooperation with others, while still enjoying the care, affection, and guidance of his parents every day. It also develops a team spirit among the youths, which is especially important from the point of view of national interest. Early every day, the boy or girl returns home to join his parents for their morning meal and either goes to school or joins them in the cultivation.

Many times, when in a jovial mood, the elders narrate stories. How they were very enterprising when they were young and slept at the Morang. The desire to have a few romantic moments with the eve spotted earlier while working grew as they attained maturity, and there was a keen competition among themselves to see who succeeded in getting the beloved.

5

EXPLOITED BY SELFISH LEADERS!

The credit for establishing schools in the initial stages and seeing a few Nagas graduating from a university outside Naga Hills goes to American Baptist missionaries. After independence, the Government of India established a chain of schools all over Naga Hills.

Under the direction of A. Z. Phizo, the hostile Nagas not only started burning down the school buildings but threatened parents with punishments ranging from fines to death if they allowed their children to continue attending school. Many Nagas who defied the threats were beaten up and heavily fined by the hostiles. An average Naga could not understand the motive behind it and felt that children should not be made to lose valuable years of their youth. The hostiles had a twofold motive. One was to prevent children from attending government-run schools, thus creating unrest among them, and the second was to induce the youth to join the hostile rank and file.

Despite the threats, fines, and kidnapping of parents and teachers by the hostiles and their confinement in the jungle, many of the villagers kept the schools open and sent their children there. Repeated warnings to students studying outside Naga Hills and their parents to discontinue education and return to Naga Hills were proved in vain, especially when the hypocrisy behind the move was fully exposed.

While the hostiles, under the directions of their leaders, pressed people to discontinue education and burned schools in Naga hills, the same leaders kept their children outside Naga hills. Not only did they ensure that their children continued their education uninterrupted, but they also provided funds to them. These funds were collected from villagers as fines, donations, and subscriptions for the hostile cause.

Children of A.Z. Phizo stayed in Shillong and continued their education uninterrupted. Phizo's Deputy Imkong Maren, vice president of Naga National Council, sent his son to Kolkata to study journalism. Imkong Maren Ao's other 2 sons, who were in jail, were released at his request to facilitate their education. Khugato Sema, a cabinet minister of the underground organization, and his brother Kaito Sema, the chief of the armed hostiles, sent their siblings to live in luxury and attend school at Shillong.

Not only these, but other underground leaders, self-styled generals, and cabinet ministers harassed, fined, and tortured students and their parents in Naga Hills, whereas they allowed their children undisturbed education outside Naga Hills. Kith and kin of Phizo and other underground hostile leaders tried day and night either for a government job or a scholarship.

For a year or so, the locals believed in the hostile propaganda and bowed to their threats. However, once the double-faced behavior of the so-called hostile leaders came to their notice, the villagers rebuilt the burned schools and gave protection to the teachers. Many young boys who were earlier allured by the hostile propaganda and had left the schools surrendered to the government to rejoin school. One and all clamored that the hostile action of burning schools and preventing the youths from attending recognized schools was nothing but an attempt to ensure that in the years to come children and relatives of hostiles who studied undisturbed during the years of unrest could claim that they were the only suitable and eligible candidates for the administrative posts. Hence, they could have easy access to the helm of the administration to dominate over others. The hostiles continued unabated efforts to prevent people from reopening the schools. Even though they killed a few teachers, villagers did not lose courage and rebuilt whatever schools had been burned.

Near Mokokchung, hostiles in large numbers raided a school in a village and tried to kidnap the teachers, causing a stir in the village. Students surrounded the teachers and ensured that the hostiles did not allow the teachers to move an inch. The womenfolk not only formed an outer ring but also stoned the hostiles. The men who were out in the fields returned upon hearing the alarm from the village tower and rushed to the spot with their spears.

The hostiles faced such an unprecedented situation, loaded their rifles, and threatened to fire, but none gave in, and the children clung to their teachers. The outnumbered hostiles fled to their jungle hideout, threatening to return with a bigger force to burn the school and kidnap the teachers. The threat never materialized.

6

DISTURBED CONDITIONS AND INTELLIGENCE RECEIVED NOT BELIEVED!

Disturbed conditions, the closure of schools for some time, and the economic deterioration forced by the hostile action had disturbed normal life, and currency had lost much of its value. Many youths were hunting for jobs, especially as their parents could not provide money to continue education in schools outside Naga Hills.

One young man who had studied up to class 7 turned up in my office and requested help in getting service. I knew his family. His father had 2 sons and landed property that yielded a fortune every year, which would keep both brothers in a flourishing condition. I drew his attention to the prosperous conditions of his family and the value of land and told him that in his life he could never earn more in service, as he could not go exceedingly high up due to a lack of education. Therefore, I advised him to stick to his father's profession as a farmer.

My words did not please him. He glanced at the well-tailored suit he was wearing and fondled his necktie. I am educated. I am a Christian, though my father is not. I can speak English. How can I dirty my hands with mud and work in the fields?

I brought to his notice cases of other Nagas who had excellent academic training and held high positions yet worked on their land in their spare time. He appeared more annoyed and replied that they were educated much earlier and not advanced.

I tried in vain to convince him of the importance of tilling land and the type of job of an exceptionally low status he could expect to get. However, he was allured by the glamour of an office and sitting on a chair to do a job of any status and by the attraction of town life. I told him to register his name with the employment exchange.

One of the noble qualities of Nagas, a virtue inherited by unsophisticated souls, is that they are neither ungrateful nor forgetful for good turns done to them. The memory of kindness extended to them remains fresh in their minds lifelong with the burning desire to make the return for it repeatedly.

In May 1956, the situation at Kohima had reached a state of high tension due to a few incidents in the surrounding areas. As people clamored for stricter security measures during the hours of darkness, a curfew was imposed from dusk to dawn in Kohima village and town except for the vehicles of pass holders and security forces. So, none moved on the roads, which were being constantly patrolled.

It was pitch dark outside. I was at my table studying reports. Twinkling stars above, lights in the distant houses, and the bright light in my room gave some relief. Except for the melodious music from the radio receiver, sounds of heavy vehicles of security forces passing intermittently on the road behind my office, the heavy boots of the patrols, and an occasional cry of a child from a nearby house, there was silence all around, which created a feeling of uncertainty.

A knock on the door to my office caused a surprise, as I had neither noticed the lights of a car approaching nor heard a sound. I peeped out of the window but could not see anyone. As the knocking was repeated, I opened the door. To my surprise, a pro-hostile leader was standing there. He said, "Good evening, I wish to meet you for urgent work," he said in one breath. Then, having walked in without awaiting my consent, he continued, "You are surprised to see me here at this hour. It is natural. You hate my sight. I know that all the officials dislike me, but I had to come. I need your help."

I replied calmly, "Your personality is not as unpleasant from my point of view as you imagine it to be. What can I do for you? Please take a seat."

"Sir, I have no time to sit. I want your help. I risked my life to come all these 6 miles through jungle routes, as I felt that you alone would help me in the hour of my need. My wife is seriously ill. She must be removed to the hospital at Imphal immediately. No officer would lend me his vehicle as none trust me. Please lend me your vehicle. It might save my wife." He was pleading with folded hands.

Surendra Mohan Kar and other members of staff, who stayed in the same building, had collected outside, having heard the sound of a stranger talking to me at that hour. My bedroom is adjacent to the office room. He requested me to go into my bedroom. One of them was standing there with a revolver in his hand. Seeing it, I signaled him to put it aside and said it is not necessary. Immediately Kar replied: "He is an extremely dangerous person. Please do not give him the vehicle; he may have some other designs."

I listened to them patiently and returned to the visitor. He was sitting there with tears in his eyes. He had overheard what my staff had said. He pleaded, 'I guarantee I will not misuse the vehicle. I will return it safely. Please save my wife's life.'

After a quick mental evaluation, I decided to give him the jeep kept at my disposal. I called the driver, gave him instructions, and then turning to the visitor, I said, "You are responsible for the safety of the driver and the vehicle. Convey my best wishes to your wife. I wish her a speedy recovery."

After he left, I informed my staff at Mao on the border of Naga Hills and Manipur and Imphal to report to me the arrival and departure of the jeep both ways as a precautionary measure. The driver and jeep returned safely at dawn and were escorted by the brother of the leader.

While he was still at Imphal, I learned that his daughter was ill. I got her admitted to a local hospital. Even my staff was confused at my action, and some who had been in Naga Hills longer than myself told me to be cautious, but I had my conviction that the individual would be a friend to me.

In the first week of June 1956, everyone in the town and village of Kohima, including armed forces, administrators, and local leaders, was busy with the impending visit of the chief of army staff General SM Srinagesh. An unprecedented reception was being staged. Information that the hostiles were planning to foil the reception was trickling in. On June 6th, just before dawn, there was a knock on the window of my bedroom; the gentleman to whom I had earlier lent the jeep was standing there. He whispered, taking precautions to save Kohima from a large raid from the hostiles, which was to coincide with the visit of the chief. Then he hurriedly left.

Due to the non-arrival of the hostile brigade from the Chakesang area, the raid was postponed, but it materialized on June 11th, 1956. I was incredibly happy with the help given by the gentleman; however, the fact that not only once but on 2 occasions, undetected, he would come during curfew hours to my office worried me, and I kept pondering over the daring nature of the individual. Except for a few bridges which are burned en route, the visit of the chief of army staff passed off successfully, and he returned happy, with many spears and shawls which had been presented to him.

I was less fortunate as I got only a few minutes to talk to him. It appeared that he was briefed by the general officer-in-charge of security forces that the backbone of the hostile Nagas had been broken and the so-called rebellion had come to an end. I could not agree and, having given all the information at hand, emphasized what was in the offing. I did not believe it, and the General Officer Commanding also left with the chief for Shillong.

It was June 11th, 1956. The whole night I was awake to ascertain how the hostile Nagas would launch the raid on Kohima at dawn. Detailed information regarding the intention and plan was available well in advance. The pattern was to be the same as adopted by the Japanese earlier. Noisy attacks from East, West, and South and a silent raid from the North on the village to occupy it. Even the villagers knew that Kohima would be raided and as a result, there was tension, especially among the loyal elements who kept on making anxious inquiries regarding protection despite repeated assurances given by the authorities.

Before the first light, I ascertained from appropriate authorities whether adequate precautions were being taken. Just then, the sound of the first shot fired by the hostiles to the South was heard. It was a signal. I was standing on the veranda of my office, watching the development, when the telephone started ringing. The Gaon Bura (elder) who stayed at the top of the village and from where he could see miles away, sent a runner to phone that the hostile Nagas were advancing in large numbers from all sides. Phone messages from the civil hospital and police reserve narrated that both places were under heavy hostile fire. The firing was increasing. Stray bullets were passing over my office.

Shri Satsuo Angami and a few Gaon Buras came running to my office to report that the hostile Nagas had already occupied half of Kohima village. Villagers were evacuating and running for their lives, and there was no trace of the security forces. Once again, I tried to contact the appropriate authorities over the phone, but failing that, gave my office jeep to them with the instructions to contact the commander of the forces personally and appraise him of this situation. Approximately 10 minutes afterwards, the commander phoned and ordered me to explain my action in sending Satsao and others who had rushed into his room. When I told him what was happening, he shouted, "Nonsense! All that you say is false. These people are creating a false alarm; there are no hostiles and Nagas anywhere near Kohima." I have ascertained from my staff officer that the sound of firing is that of the Assam Rifles conducting classification of recruits on the range. I tried to tell him the truth but in vain.

A few minutes thereafter, the officer commanding the police station, which is in the heart of the town, phoned and reported that the whole village was occupied by the hostile Nagas and the police station was under fire. Soon, the stray bullets were hitting the roof of the commander officer's residence. By the afternoon, the whole town and camp of Assam Rifles was flooded with evacuees from the Kohima village. The Deputy Commissioner of Kohima came to my office, and we stood on the veranda watching and discussing the situation. From there, we went to the mission compound along with the Superintendent of Police and the Commandant of the 3rd Battalion Assam Rifles to get more information and to watch the advance by a unit of security forces to clear the hostiles from the village.

The situation remained confused. At 4:00 PM, the local commander called a conference of all the services. I was also invited. The officer-in-charge of advancing troops turned up at the conference with exhibits that included bibles, schoolbooks (both used and unused), and women's clothing, which were believed to have been recovered from an underground shelter overrun by them.

He reported that there are no Naga hostiles in the area. "Look at these articles found in the dugout. It is the work of the locals," he said. He was supported by the commander, but no one could explain why they would not advance more than 200 yards during the whole day. The climax came in the evening, just before dusk, when the curfew was to come into force; a young Naga couple approached me with a request. They said, "We were married yesterday at noon. The Assam Rifles camp is overflowed with displaced persons from the village and there is no place. Please help us and get us some accommodation." It was difficult, though not an impossible task, and a place was found for them.

The night of June 11th was unnerving; no one could say what was happening. The sound of firing didn't stop until dawn. The whole night I was awake, due to constant phone calls from all quarters to inquire what was happening. At midnight, there was a heavy burst of bullets on the roof of my office-cum-residence. Everyone appeared to be in a panic. I walked from room to room encouraging my staff to remain calm. To my surprise, one of the outstation staff who compared himself with King Kong was sleeping on the ground, with the mattress and cot turned over him. We asked him what his intention was; he replied from inside, "I am a big target and could be easily hit so I am under an improvised bulletproof shelter." His answer brought a burst of laughter from all, a light moment! I went out to see how the unarmed constables on duty outside were doing! Angame, who was supposed to be on duty at that hour, was fast asleep in the jeep under the influence of rice beer.

7

NEED FOR THE RIGHT EXPOSURE
AND GUIDANCE

My friends in Naga Hills often pressed me to bring my family to Kohima. Besides the lack of accommodation, the difficulty which confronted me was the education of my children. My wife was not a stranger to Naga Hills. She had accompanied me to Kohima in 1952 and 1954. The locals even volunteered to build a suitable accommodation as the government had plans to build an office cum residential accommodation for me and my staff, but this had not materialized so far.

Finally bowing to their pressure, I brought my family to Kohima during the winter vacation in 1957. Despite the discomfort, we settled down in a room within my office. My son Rajeev, a fiery lad of 5 years, and daughter Bhagyashree, a few years older than him, soon became one with the locals with their love for food from the region. Despite warnings by the higher military and the civil authorities, we went to different places in the interiors, accompanied and unescorted as was my practice.

As my wife and I strolled in the yard of my office-cum-residence one early morning, I narrated to her the different aspects of Naga life and their sterling qualities. How, despite being intelligent and politically conscious, they were ignorant of many things outside Naga Hills due to the fact that many had not crossed the boundary of the district.

My wife then reminded me, "You were telling me about the Naga gentleman who had come to invite us for dinner, and about his change of attitude." I said yes, and narrated to her the story of his life. He was a well-educated and enthusiastic follower of A. Z. Phizo.

When about 40 years old, he went to see Calcutta. One early morning, as he walked on the Main Street of Calcutta accompanied by a local guide, he was amazed at the sights! The building structures, shops, offices, and the thousands of people who moved on foot, in cars, buses, tram cars, cycles, horse-drawn coaches, and. Tired, he stopped, and it was already evening, and sat down on the pavement! He asked his guide, "How many streets are there?" "Many," replied the guide. "How many people stay in Calcutta?" he asked. "Many millions," the guide replied.

When the traveler returned to Kohima, he decided to break with Phizo, as he thought of the millions of people of different faiths and from different parts of India living in one town harmoniously, under one banner. Many foreigners from other nations mingled with them peacefully. "Here in Nagaland not one of us, 250,000 Nagas, possesses a car. We have no communication system, and one is tired of fighting with another." He thought it was not suitable to ask for this imaginary independence and disturb our lives. He said, "I am out! I want to support the government and derive the best advantage for my people through cooperation."

As we were talking and waiting for our children to join us at breakfast, a Naga youth walked up. Having greeted us, he declared his intention to seek compensation for the loss suffered by him during his return journey from Jorhat.

I remembered that he was a representative of the church who had traveled with the pass issued by me. The rebel Nagas created trouble in the border areas. Everyone who went out of Naga Hills was a suspect and was often detained and interrogated. However, those who carried the pass from the administration or from my office had no difficulty.

The youth had taken a pass from my office and gone to Jorhat to attend a church meeting. During the return journey, all his belongings were stolen, and he was claiming the cost of lost articles. Having consoled him, I asked him how I was responsible for the loss and how he had presumed that it was obligatory on my part to compensate him.

He replied, "Sir, your pass was honored by everyone." At Dimapur, I was stopped by the police, and as soon as I showed the pass, the officer said, "It is the pass issued by Lt Col Pandit, let him go, he must be a good man." On the train and at Jorhat, the pass worked like magic, and I enjoyed full freedom of movement. However, during the journey, I went to sleep. I had purchased clothes and other requirements worth Rs.180 and kept them under the berth. Someone stole these at night. "You must pay me the cost because I had your pass. Even the police and military did not attempt to stop me because of it. Then how could someone dare steal all my belongings?"

We were amused by his argument. My wife couldn't check herself and laughed. She said, "How simple and innocent these people are. How will you solve this problem?" Without replying to my wife, I turned to the boy and patted him on his back. "I am indeed sorry for the loss. I know you must be feeling it in these difficult times."

His face brightened. "I asked him, did you show the pass to the thief?" "How could I?" he replied, "I was asleep." Well, then how was he to know that you had a pass issued by me? Don't you think that if you had shown the pass to him, he would not have done such a daring thing, as did the police and military. He would not have committed the theft of your belongings.

The boy was convinced. "Yes, what you say is true, it is my mistake. I did not let him know that I had a pass. Sorry that I troubled you." He wished both of us a good day and left uncompensated yet content. Such was the innocence.

At the request of the Nagas, who were being harassed by the hostile elements, troops were dispatched to the Naga Hills. It included a unit of the Sikh regiment. Their arrival indeed caused a great stir among most of the Nagas who had, for the first time, seen the sturdy and tall Sikh with a turban and beard. A few days after their arrival, a member of the Gaon Bura and other elders came to my office with the request for an interview with the General Commanding Officer.

When I asked them the purpose of the interview, they said that they wanted to request the General Officer Commanding to replace the battalion of the Sikh Regiment with some other troops. I was surprised by their curious request and told them that not only were the troops well-disciplined and well-behaved, but they also had the highest traditions and were the best fighters.

The spokesperson replied, "They are good, no one will dispute it, but you know, Sir, in Naga Hills the fair sex outnumbers the other. We were also young and full of mischief, yet we have seen British and American troops stationed here during the war and how they attracted the fair sex. It is better that they would be replaced by Ghurkha or any other troops without a beard."

I was puzzled on how to deal with their persistent demand. Having promised them an interview with the General Officer Commanding, I asked, "Do you think that the Gurkhas and others may be timid and keep away from the advances of the girls?" "No, Sir," said this spokesperson emphatically. "But if children are born from them, no one will know the origin; in case of Sikhs, everyone will know." Still puzzled by the argument, I asked him how?

The spokesman said, embarrassed, "They will be born with a beard." To that, all burst out laughing to the great embarrassment of my visitors. Finally, I controlled my laughter about their simplicity and innocence on matters beyond their understanding. I asked them to get on 2 vehicles, took them to the headquarters of the Sikh regiment, and showed them that many of the young Sikh boys had no beard. Then I asked, "Do you still want to see the commanding general officer?" They shook their heads in the negative. The people had little exposure, and their minds were untainted.

8

CONTINUED CONTACT WITH SENSITIVE HOSTILES ESSENTIAL!

My talk with many of the local Nagas and villagers made me conclude that, though a few were certain of their demand for independence, others were not sure what they meant by it and why the armed rebellion was undertaken by some of their leaders. However, one thing was sure: everyone was tired of the violence and was eager that peace must be restored immediately in the Naga Hills.

To assess their mood, I undertook an extensive tour of villages in the interior in the first half of 1957. I was not only surprised but amused by their ideas and expressions, which indicated not only their simplicity and ignorance of worldly affairs but also anything beyond their horizon and frontiers.

Ninety percent of the Nagas understood independence as separation from Assam. When I asked who would grant them independence, they replied, "U.N.O. and Prime Minister Shri Nehru."

When I asked what the U.N.O. was and where it was located, some replied that the U.N.O. was in Delhi and the Prime Minister of India was the President of it, and a few replied that the U.N.O. and Prime Minister Shri Nehru were identical. They also emphasized that it was Mahatma Gandhi and Shri Jawaharlal Nehru whom they respected the most, and it was for the latter to establish peace in the Naga Hills.

During my tour, I was surprised to read a propaganda leaflet issued under the signature of Krisanisa Agami, Kodaghey (President) of the so-called hostile Naga.

The Federal Authority stated that a meeting of the U.N.O. was held in Delhi, attended by representatives of all nations, including the President of the United States of America and the Prime Minister of the United Kingdom. The meeting considered the Nagas' demand and concluded that it was correct. They approached the Prime Minister of India, but Shri Nehru got angry. Not only did he question their authority to hold a meeting without his permission, but he kicked them out of New Delhi. Nagas should not worry about failure. Now the U.N.O. would hold a meeting outside India, and the demand of Nagas would be granted.

Yet another leaflet stated that some of their leaders had gone to Pakistan and Burma and would soon return with independence. I brought the leaflets and gave them to their leaders at Kohima. They said, "Ignorance. We do not know what the U.N.O. is and we talk of it."

Nagas are very suspicious of non-Nagas, but it is equally true that fair dealings, sympathetic treatment, and adherence to the words earn their faith and loyalty. Though I had neither administrative powers nor the authority of the operational commander, yet due to my 'missionary' attitude, I had the privilege of gaining their faith and respect. This was experienced on many occasions.

Five days had passed after the Kohima raid, but still, all means of line and land communication to Kohima were cut off. I had no opportunity to serve during the siege of Kohima by the Japanese in World War II, but the accounts I had read of it were brought to vivid reality by the present situation.

Fighting continued all around Kohima. Even without binoculars, one could see the hostile Nagas moving on hills surrounding Kohima.

Surendra Mohan Kar and I were in the office discussing and assessing the reports and devising means and ways to tide over the difficulties when the constable on duty announced the arrival of a Naga who desired an immediate hearing. It was my policy not to keep anyone who came to see me waiting. Experience had taught me that a tribal was very touchy about the delay.

Even though the matter may be a very trivial one like the loss of a pig or a dog, to him it was of paramount importance. He desired immediate hearing at any hour of the day and night and became impatient and annoyed if there was a delay. He was not worried about the outcome and the result, but he was content if he got a patient hearing and sympathetic treatment as soon as he arrived.

I had earlier met the young Naga who walked in. After discharge from the army, he had come to Kohima and had reported his arrival to me. He hailed from the Ao tribe. He had married an Angami girl on the 8th of June. As soon as he entered, he excitedly said in Hindi, "You must help me."

Trying to calm him, I asked what had happened and what help I could give him. Still agitated, he spoke, "You know, Sir, I got married on the 8th, but only after 3 days, I had to leave the village with my wife and mother-in-law when the hostile Nagas occupied it. Now we are in the Assam Rifles camp, we have no privacy. You must help me."

"It is your domestic affair. I cannot perceive how I can help you and in what way," I asked. Promptly, he replied, "You must get us privacy." I could not help laughing at his innocence, but Surendra Kar lost his temper. He pounced on him, shouting, "Do we undertake such tasks and work? What do you think this office is for?"

Scared, the youth was about to make good his escape when I asked him to wait and asked Kar to sit down. Addressing Kar, I said, "Don't lose your temper. He has come with the hope that we may solve his problem. Let us hear him and consider whether we can help him." Then turning to the lad, I said, "Probably you have misunderstood. The Assam Rifles lines are flooded with evacuees from the village; hence, there is no privacy."

Before I could say anything further, he replied, "That is not the case. I have friends in the Assam Rifles, and so I can have a room to myself. But my mother-in-law will not allow my wife to come. Now she wants her to be married to a Non-Commissioned Officer of the Assam Rifles, and so is persuading her not to live with me. You must help me. I must have my wife!"

I thought it over and told him, "I am afraid I cannot ask your wife directly to do what you wish, as I am sure she will not obey my orders. But I will send Kephelou to ascertain if what you say is correct. And if she is happy with you and willing to continue as your wife, he will bring her near the Assam Rifles Camp. Outside the camp, hundreds of villagers from Kohima are staying in the huts built on agricultural land meant for those guarding the crop. You can stay there and with time, your mother-in-law's efforts to separate you 2 will cease. Meanwhile, at a suitable opportunity, you make your way to your home in the Ao Area."

He appeared to be contented and left with Kephelou Angami, who was briefed by me. After some days, Kephelou returned and reported that the happy couple had left to take abode in the Kheti huts. A couple of days later, the bridegroom turned up to thank me. "My wife and I will never forget all the good you have done for us. You are our father hence onwards. We will do anything for you," he said. He kept his word and helped me despite the danger to his own life until normalcy returned to Kohima, and then left with his wife for the Ao area.

Kohima village was cleared of the hostiles and resettled with normal life. I was busy at the desk when Kephelou Angami announced the arrival of a Naga gentleman and a girl who urgently wanted to meet me. I told him to bring them in. Just after Kephelou crossed the door, the gentleman hurriedly walked in. I knew him well, and he had been selected for an important government post and was likely to join in a month. He came close to me, folded his hands, and whispered, "You have to save my reputation and happiness." Before I could ask him what had happened, he hurried back and drew the curtain across the door, asking the girl to come in.

I had not seen her in town but did not know who she was. He walked with her and introduced her to me as his fiancée. I greeted her and offered her a chair. Both sat, but the gentleman placed his chair a little behind. When I asked what I could do for them, tears rolled down her cheeks. Wiping them with her handkerchief, she said, "I want justice from you." Emotion prevented her from further speech.

Starting in a low and calm voice, the gentleman said, "Sir, we have been engaged for over 2 years and are to wed in the coming winter. For the last few days, I have been very busy with my appointment and related subjects, which prevented me from meeting her. Yesterday evening, when I called on her, she accused me of going around with other girls and declared her intention to break off the engagement. I pleaded with her. Ultimately, she decided that she would marry me if you advised her to do so."

I was surprised to hear it. Never, even in my dreams, had I believed that I would have to tackle such a problem! Turning to her, I asked if she had anything to say. Her answer, interspersed with sobbing, was, "I loved him. Even now, I do love him. But I have heard that he is flirting with other girls. I want you to tell me the truth and advise me. You know and understand the Nagas individually, and each one of us has faith in you. To me, you are a true minister and God who knows everything and advises best. What shall I do?"

The suspicions of the girl were not groundless, yet it was a fact that the man wanted to marry her and no one else. He had told me so very often. Still, his sitting there with folded hands and pleading eyes could not induce me to tell a lie. "Well," I said reassuringly, "I know one thing well, and that is, despite your suspicions, he is not interested in anyone else from a matrimonial point of view. He always hoped to make you his life partner."

The young woman blushed with happiness and joy. She wiped her tears with a smile on her face. Her eyes shot a shy glance at her fiancé as she got up from the chair. Rising from the chair, he thanked me, then took her arm and tenderly said, "Now you must never, never doubt me again."

She came forward with him, arm in arm, and asked for my blessings. I blessed them, and they walked out hand in hand. Since then, I have had many occasions to meet the couple at their place of posting in the interior.

9

NOTHING IS INSIGNIFICANT IN GRIM TIMES

Khonoma village, home of Angami Zapu Phizo, the rebel leader, and Krisanisa Angami, the so-called President of the rebel Naga Federal Authority, was a place of prestige for both the hostiles and the government. Especially since Thevouma, one of the 3 Khels (suburbs), vehemently opposed A.Z. Phizo and his supporters' activities. The 2 Khels that supported the hostiles time and again carried out heavy attacks on Thevouna. The people of Thevouna refused to evacuate, and despite heavy losses, held their ground to the last.

One of the elders lost all his sons in the fighting. When his last son was killed, his daughter-in-law was pregnant, and that was the only hope the elder cherished to continue the heritage. In due time, she gave birth to a male child, to the great rejoicing of the clan. The delivery took place at midnight, but unfortunately, the mother expired an hour thereafter, leaving the child in the care of the grandfather of the elders. The grandfather went to the nearest military camp and phoned me for help. At my request, the Commanding Officer of the unit sent his medical officer to render help. From Kohima, a special vehicle was sent carrying powdered milk tins, nourishing food, and medicines for the child.

I visited the place after a few months. To my surprise, a big gathering of men, women, and children was waiting for me at the entrance to the village, which had become a fort and bore the marks of heavy fighting. As I discussed, the elder took me straight to his house. The old lady was sitting near the fireplace with the child in her lap, surrounded by kith and kin and the village defense guards.

One of the elderly ladies placed an Angami shawl on my shoulders and offered Madhu (rice beer). The elder spoke, "We respect you more than our father and mother. You know us, understand us, God has sent you as His representative to this house. I have lost all my children. Here is the man in infancy to carry forward the name of my family and that of my 3 sons, who gave their lives to keep off the tyranny of Zapu Phizo and his followers. Bless my grandson that he may grow to be a healthy, strong, and powerful man to carry on the traditions and customs set forth by his elders and keep the flag of India flying in this place forever."

It was a new experience for me. Despite a few gray hairs, I never had thought that I had achieved the status and position to bless on such solemn occasions. My parents were alive, and I looked to them for blessings and guidance, and consequently, I still felt like a child having the patronage of loving parents.

Realizing the situation, I stood up solemnly and prayed to Almighty God to let me be blessed on His behalf. Then, touching the head of the child, I said, "May God make this child grow to manhood to fulfill the wishes of his grandparents." There was great rejoicing among the inmates of the house. I drank the full glass of Madhu to relieve myself of the tension I had undergone.

During the Naga Peoples Convention in Kohima, the place was flooded with people and vehicles. Immediately after the convention was over, an old Angami woman came to my office with a lengthy petition requesting compensation for her dog that had been run over by one of the vehicles. Despite the heavy pressure of work and the rush of visitors, I spared time to meet her. Old and wrinkled, she was supported by her daughter. Taking great pains to explain her petition, she said that she was a poor widow with the liability of 4 children and had purchased the pup for a rupee and brought it up. The children loved the dog, and she had also hoped that the dog would make a good dish on the occasion of her daughter's marriage. She had approached everyone, military and civil authorities for investigation and compensation, but they had not only completely ignored her but laughed at her.

The loss of a small dog was a very small matter, and the authorities concerned could not be blamed for disregarding her, as they were busy with serious and important matters. Yet her sorrow was genuine, and her loss a paramount one from her point of view. Therefore, I paid her 10 rupees, and she left contented.

A few days after my visit to Khonoma, the elder who had lost 3 sons fighting the hostiles came to meet me at Kohima. He desired a patient hearing, as he wanted to confide in me. I closed the door, and both of us sat down on the sofa.

He started narrating the history of his family and Khel and how they had opposed Angami Zapu Phizo from the beginning. The Naga National Council was formed for the welfare and well-being of the Nagas and was purely a social organization. Mondonemo Lotha and Visier Angami, the Presidents in succession, kept up the original character of the organization, but Zapu Phizo, who became President by defeating Visier Angami by one vote, turned it into a political organization dominated by Nagas who had been converted to Christianity and were more educated.

Most of the people from the elders' khel were non-Christians and as such they were looked down upon and treated differently by Zapu Phizo and the 2 Khels under his influence. The khel, Thevoma, did not approve of Phizo's activities and kept aloof, remaining loyal to the Government. The result was obvious, and they were neglected by both sides. Only 3 men from their khel reached the middle-school stage, the others remaining illiterate. When the disturbances commenced in Naga Hills, the 2 Khels loyal to Phizo left the village and, supported by the hostiles from other areas, launched successive raids on Thevouma Khel who remained in the village,

The Thevouma held their ground till the last, despite heavy casualties suffered by them. The elder who had lost his 3 sons wanted to avenge their deaths now. As he now had a grandson to carry forward the name of his family, he was free to carry out the desire of his heart, which was to avenge the death of his 3 sons.

If the elder took the heads of the murderers of his 3 sons, his grandson was free! If not, it would become his responsibility. Hence, he wanted to spare his grandson from this ordeal! He had collected evidence as to who had killed his sons. For hours, I tried to persuade him to give up the idea, telling him that when normalcy returned, the offenders would most probably repent, and his desire could be fulfilled by other lenient means for which provisions existed. At last, he agreed, and so I requested him to take an oath to that effect.

Nagas have their own code of conduct and justice. Normally, beheading a murderer is justified if not settled earlier by other means. If the next of kin cannot avenge the death, the burden of revenge is carried on for generations until it is accomplished. In 1955, I came across a case where a dispute between 2 Naga families had resulted in a murder 5 generations ago. These families were subsequently separated during the separation of Burma from India. However, a descendant of the murderer's family, who had probably forgotten the incident and gone to live in Burma, was murdered by the aggrieved family.

Often, murders resulted in head-hunting and even the massacre of the whole village. The last one was in 1955 in Tuensang Frontier Division when, over the murder of a dak runner from their village by the hostiles of Yempang village, the affected villagers raided the village of the hostiles and took the head of each man, woman, and child.

Customs and the traditional way of justice do provide other lenient means of settling such disputes, provided the offender takes the initiative and comes forward with repentance. In such a case, the dispute could be settled either over a glass of Madhu or by compensation in kind or cash. Nagas can brood over injustice and take revenge someday, but at the same time, they have a unique quality of generosity and broad-heartedness, and they can quickly forgive and forget.

Taking an oath is a solemn custom among Nagas and is strictly adhered to, even at the cost of one's life. The severity of the oath depends upon the type, and it includes taking an oath from cutting a tiger's head to a cat's head. But the elder took his oath on one condition. He said, "You are father and mother to me. I take an oath and promise that as long as you are with us on this Naga Land soil, I will do nothing against your wishes and as directed, I will not kill those who murdered my sons."

When I was about to leave Kohima forever, the elder and his wife came to meet me with their grandson, who was nearly 2 years of age and healthy. I presented him with a few articles as a memory. The elder was overwhelmed with emotion. He came forward and said, "I must tell you that I want to save my grandson from the ordeal of taking revenge for the death of his father and uncles. I am old and have enjoyed life to the fullest and suffered the worst. I can avenge their death easily and endure subsequent punishment in court. I took an oath and was bound to you. You are leaving the Naga land soil, and so the oath exists no more."

I argued with him in vain. He stood firm. "I was conditionally bound to you. If you stay with us, I will adhere to the oath and make my grandson abide by it forever. If you leave this soil, the oath will cease to be operative, and I will do what I have said."

I had to leave, and a few months later, I learned that the elder had avenged the death of his sons. He had shot dead in the jungle those who had killed his sons, severed their heads, and then reported the fact to the administration himself. Placed behind bars, he went to sleep happily without the customary Madhu or rohi. The next morning, he woke up joyful. "Never in my life did I feel so relieved, happy, and fresh as I do," he said. "For the first time in 3 long years, I have had sound sleep!"

10

IMPULSIVE AND VINDICTIVE!

Nagas work hard and also like entertainment and enjoyment. But they are often casual in love! Couples who are wed in the evening may separate even before the dawn of the next day.

Everyone in the Naga Hills knew Shri Satsuo Angami of Kohima, who served meritoriously as a Junior Commissioned Officer in the Indian Army. He was my guest in 1951 at Shillong. When I asked him, before he went to bed, what time he would like to have his cup of tea the next morning, he replied, "At 4:30 am. Add 2 pegs of rum, but no milk or sugar."

In the Naga Hills, the majority of people start the day with Madhu (rice beer), which is a nourishing diet. Men and women proceeding to the fields early in the morning carrying jars of Madhu in their baskets are a common sight. Only a few Nagas who have embraced Christianity do not touch liquor of any kind, including Madhu or Rohi. Men returning home after the day's work normally spend the evening at the common meeting ground of each Khel drinking Madhu, smoking, and gossiping. Shri Satsuo Angami was not an exception to this way of life.

A few months before he was shot dead by hostile Nagas while holding a meeting of the village Panchayat in his house after dusk, which is in the heart of the town and adjacent to the Police Station, Shri Vikrulie Angami, who was Satsuo's best friend, came to my place to inform me that Satsuo and Shrimati Satsuo had a quarrel late in the evening, and in a fit of anger, they had decided to end their wedded life, and Shrimati Satsuo had left their home. The cause of the Angamis' quarrel was a woman's jealousy. Angami's efforts to prevent them from separating were in vain, so he had come to solicit my help. He refused to leave my office until I promised to take steps to reunite them.

I was rather perturbed and sent for Satsuo and spoke to him. Then I went across to the house where Shrimati Satsuo was temporarily residing. From their talks, I concluded that during a heated argument under the influence of Madhu, both had taken a hasty step, and they had realized their mistake the next dawn. Yet, neither was prepared to step forward and take the initiative to forgive and forget. Each wanted the other to express his or her repentance.

Both the government and their society looked up to Satsuo as an elder of standing. I had to do something quickly so that they were not separated forever. I requested them to meet me at the house they had occupied during the peak of the disturbance, and they agreed. They were escorted there by Shri and Shrimati Vikrulie, who then withdrew, leaving them in my charge. Addressing both jokingly, I asked if they would hear me patiently. Then I reminded Shrimati Satsuo of an incident that took place just after the Naga People's Convention.

Resolutions passed by the Naga People's Convention held at Kohima in 1957 were accepted by the government, and an era of the new administration was expected. A team of 4 high dignitaries from the Government of India was touring Naga Hills to work out requirements. A reception was accorded to them by the elders of Kohima village, and I was there sitting in a corner, watching. Shrimati Satsuo Angami approached the senior-most member of the visitors.

Having apologized to them for raising the subject and requesting them not to misunderstand her, she asked their permission to offer Madhu first to "Baba" (father) before it was offered to them as a mark of respect. Having obtained their assent, she returned to fill the glasses. I was surprised at the new procedure adopted as it was unusual and was wondering about it when she walked up to me. Holding the glass in front of me, she said, "First, we must honor our Baba, and then others, however highly placed they may be." I felt embarrassed and requested her to offer it first to the visitors.

"She was adamant. Satsuo and a few elders also joined Shrimati Satsuo and pressed me to accept the glass. Confused, I turned to Shri S.M. Dutt, who was sitting with the visitors. He and Shri Sarin I.C.S., who was the spokesman for the visitors, signaled me to take the glass."

After reminding her about the incident, I asked whether her words were true even that day. Both shouted, "True! It will never change. You are our baba." Both had a relaxed attitude, and the tension visible in the beginning had disappeared.

I opened my haversack and handed over a bottle of beer to Satsuo and one of rum to Shrimati Satsuo. I then said very gently, "Take the advice of your baba. All people look to you for guidance. You both like each other." Then turning to each one, I pleaded on behalf of the other. Both burst out laughing. They exchanged the bottles and shook hands. As I was about to leave, both caught hold of me. "Baba, sit down. Share our joy of reunion."

11

THE STRIFE: YOUTHS SUFFERED AND WERE MISGUIDED

In early May 1956, while going through the list of detainees in Kohima Jail, I noticed that several youths who were students at colleges and schools were imprisoned there. I knew some of them, and the parents of others had been pleading repeatedly for their release.

I interviewed each one of them and prepared a brief, which I used to petition the authorities for their release. While some were released unconditionally, the authorities insisted on securities and guarantees for others. I convinced their relatives, as well as some of my friends among the Nagas, to stand bail for them.

I had a firm belief, following my talk with the individuals, that after their release, they would stand by their words and continue their education peacefully without indulging in politics until their graduation. All of them, except one whom I trusted most, kept their word and joined schools and colleges at Shillong and other places outside Naga Hills. The one who strayed informed me by post that he had been kidnapped by the hostiles. But subsequently, I learned that he had gone underground to join the hostiles.

I was indeed upset by his lack of candor, especially as, having gone underground, he had proved a great asset to the hostile Nagas, and the authorities concerned time and again blamed me for having pressed for his release. In addition, those who stood security for him were being pressed by the authorities, and they, in turn, harassed me to do something to relieve them of the danger. I somehow felt convinced that the individual would realize his folly and would return.

A year later, I was touring the defector's AO area. When I visited a friend's house, I found a kit lying there, which I learned belonged to this boy. I left a note on his kit with the following words: "May God bless you. Those who stood security for you at my instructions are on the verge of taking your place in jail. I also feel betrayed by your behavior."

The next day, when I reached Mokokchung, I got a long letter from him apologizing for his behavior and requesting me to visit his house in a nearby village where his mother would offer me a Naga Shawl as a token of his respect. I did visit his house and met his mother to pay my respects to her but did not accept the shawl. I told his mother what had happened and that I could not accept the shawl until he left the hostiles and joined school again to keep the word he had given me.

Surprisingly enough, he did come to meet me. I was in Shillong at the time. In fact, he had gone to Kohima to meet me and had followed me to Shillong. Never again did he return to join the hostiles.

During one of my tours in the Naga Hills, I entered a village and was talking to the locals when an old Naga woman approached me, requesting an interview. I went to her house with an interpreter, and after offering me a seat, she asked me if I still remembered one of my old friends. On hearing his name, I was surprised and astonished at the question. I told her that I knew him well and longed to meet him but had learned that he had joined the hostiles, which had perturbed me. I inquired about what he was doing and where he was.

She replied, "I am his mother. He has been appointed as the Health Minister of the so-called Naga Federal Authority, but for over a month, he has been lying ill in the jungle without any medical help. He cannot get any medicines. He heard that you are coming to our village and has expressed a desire to meet you."

I was happy at the opportunity of meeting an old acquaintance, especially as he was ill and needed help. Earlier, when he was in a perturbed mood, I had advised and guided him. I offered to go to his jungle hideout to meet him, but she told me not to do so. Explaining her reluctance, she said, "I am not worried about you. I know that no one will harm you. We all, those who are not hostiles, as well as the hostile Nagas, like and respect you. My son is not far away. He is within an hour's walk. But your visit may place him under suspicion and his life may be in danger. The hostile Nagas of another tribe are camping very near to him against our wishes, and they are without an elderly leader who can restrict their actions. Though a friend, you are known for your official assignment. Please do not visit him." "I will bring him to the roadside. He is too weak even to walk. He is my son. I wish him to live. He told me to arrange this meeting with you so that you can take him with you and put him on the right path. I will bring him to the roadside, and then you can take him under your care."

I arranged for an ambulance to pick him up, but in the evening, the old woman came to my camp in the next village to inform me that the hostiles of other tribes smelled foul play as I was on tour in the area, and her son would not allow himself to leave the place. The next day, I departed from the area, leaving a vehicle in a nearby camp to pick him up. The trick worked. He was allowed to be shifted to his house for better comfort. From there, he came to Kohima. On seeing me, he shouted, "I am sure I will survive now. Forgive and forget what I did. Save me and send me to Shillong to continue my education." I feel so happy to see him prospering as a postgraduate student.

12

CONFUSING AND TRAGIC TIMES, AND ABOUT 2 MOTHERS

The schools in Kohima were closed in June 1956 due to the disturbances. The students were roaming about. Every day, there would be students approaching me with a request to arrange a seat for them in some school outside Naga Hills.

One of the girl students who was staying with some boys on the outskirts of Kohima town and had disappeared during the Kohima raid reappeared and was arrested on suspicion. I was not aware of it until a youth whom I had known well turned up. He narrated the arrest of the girl and then requested me to help him in getting her released.

I was eager to know why he was interested in her and the reasons why he pressed for her release. From his answers, I could make out that for some years he and some other boys from his area had stayed with her in a privately arranged boarding. She had fed them well, and she was like a sister to him. I was not satisfied with his answers and felt that he was hiding something. However, since he insisted that she was like a sister to him, I decided to give him the benefit of the doubt and was about to call the officer-in-charge at the Police Station when Amal Roy walked in. He informed me that a girl who had been arrested earlier in the day had requested an interview with me, and hence she was sent under an escort to my office.

A young girl of about eighteen years of age walked in. Having made her sit next to the youth, I asked her reasons for coming to see me. She promptly replied, "I was in Kohima but during the raid by the hostiles, I went to stay in the Kheti huts. I returned in search of my husband but was arrested. I have nothing to do with the hostile Nagas."

When I questioned her as to who her husband was, she pointed out the youth sitting next to her. "What!" I exclaimed. "He is your husband! But he says that you are his sister." I then asked the youth to explain. He continued to insist that she was his sister, whereas she emphasized that she was his wife.

As he would not accept and agree to what she said, she lost her temper and walked up to Amal Roy standing near the desk. Taking his hand, she said to the youth, "So I am your sister! I will marry Roy."

Before she could say anything further, the youth walked up to her and forced her into the chair, saying, "Roy is a good man. Do not ruin him also. Be content with me only." He then requested her release again. I told him that I could not help him unless he came out with the truth regarding his relationship with her.

For a minute, he stood there with his head bent. Then he said slowly, "I felt ashamed to tell you of our relationship. Our marriage has not been solemnized, but we lived as husband and wife for convenience."

I arranged for her release, and he stood security for her. Two days later, the officer-in-charge of the police station informed me that both the youth and the girl had disappeared. I instructed my staff to make inquiries, but both could not be traced. I came under heavy criticism from the protectors of law and order for having recommended the release of the girl. Indeed, I did not know the girl well, but I trusted the youth fully and knew that he had faith in me. I wanted the youth to continue his education.

A few months later, I received a letter from him. He informed me that his so-called wife had intoxicated him and then tempted him to go out for a walk in the moonlight. When they crossed the town's boundary, she handed him over to a hostile, uneducated leader who needed an English-speaking secretary. The hostile leader made him sign a bond pledging the life of his father if he deserted. He was tired of living in the jungle and was worried about the interruption in his education.

He wanted to return, but if he surrendered of his own accord, the life of his father would be in danger. Hence, he wanted to be arrested and released on bail. He would be awaiting arrest in a house in a certain village near an army post, and the house would have a red and white cloth tied to the pole in front on a certain specified day.

Security forces obliged me by arresting the youth. Administrative authorities helped release him on bail, and he was sent to Shillong to continue his education. His friends teased him time and again about being kidnapped by a girl who was his sister and wife for convenience's sake. The girl in question ran after him no more! She had died before he was arrested.

During the spate of surrenders, my office had a very busy time. I had returned after a flying visit to my home in Nagpur. My mother, who was seriously ill for over 6 months, had passed away a few days after I reached home. Though the work kept me engrossed, often her memory overpowered my thoughts.

One afternoon, I was not in the mood to meet anyone. Probably, it was the first time in many years that sentiments had overpowered my mind, and I was not inclined to do anything. I closed the door of my office and instructed the constables on duty to inform all the visitors that I was not in.

I sat near the window, looking at the beautiful hills of the Zapukong Range in the south and thinking of the days when my mother had cared for me. The hills towering over one another reminded me of the magnitude and solidarity of my mother's mind and heart. She had been ill for many days and was eager to meet me, but work prevented me from going. I left only when I got a frantic message. She was unconscious when I reached, but on hearing my voice regained consciousness. Even the doctors were surprised at the turn in her condition, but it did not last long. Wherever I was posted, whenever I got leave, I always went home to visit my parents first and spent a major part of the leave with them. Now, father was still alive, but home in the real sense had disappeared. The weather changed and it started drizzling. I felt the sky shared my sorrow and was shedding tears along with me.

Just then, the non-Naga constable who was on duty entered through the back door to tell me that an extremely old Naga woman had been waiting for over 2 hours to meet me. I sent for Kephelou Angami and told him to find out who she was, what she wanted, and whether it was urgent. Kephelou returned running. "Sir, she is Angami Zapu Phizo's mother. After her surrender, she was brought here, and she would like to meet you!"

I was surprised to hear that the mother of A.Z. Phizo was outside. Out of curiosity and respect for age, I went out. There she was, an old woman of 80, who appeared very weak and was dressed in torn clothes. As it was drizzling, I asked Khephelou to take her to the visitors' room and asked her if I could do anything for her. She replied through Kephelou that she had surrendered and, on arrival at Kohima, had come to report to me. I told her that I had nothing to ask her because of her age and physical condition, and despite her being the mother of A.Z. Phizo, the rebel leader in exile, she was free to go to any place and live anywhere unrestricted, provided the district authorities had no objection to it.

She was shivering with cold, so I gave her a Naga shawl that someone had given me, and also gave her the 10 rupees she had requested. I then sent for Dr. Iralu, her son-in-law, and he took her home in the jeep provided by my office. It turned out that A.Z. Phizo and Mrs. Iralu were her children from a second marriage, and she had a son from her first marriage. The next day, she sent me a message requesting a vehicle to come to my office, as she was too weak to walk. I was surprised and wondered why she wanted to see me again.

When she arrived, she sat down in a chair, and tears filled her eyes. She expressed her gratitude for the kindness and good treatment she had received, especially given that her son had started a rebellion against the government. She then shared how the villagers who had left their homes at the instigation of her son were suffering in the jungle, which she too had experienced. She expressed her desire to issue an appeal to all Nagas residing in the jungle to return home and live peacefully. Her son-in-law dictated her appeal in English and Angami.

Then she asked her son-in-law to convey to me her sorrow and grief at the news that my mother had passed away and that she would always consider me as her son henceforth for the affection shown to her. I thanked her as she left. I thought a great deal about the psychological aspect of her gesture. I considered myself lucky that I could receive affection, love, and respect from old and young among the Nagas. Was it my personality or behavior toward others or the missionary attitude in my subconscious mind?

A few days earlier, I had read an appeal issued by the late Shri Govind Vallabh Pant, the Home Minister, calling upon government servants to adopt a missionary attitude, not only dedicating themselves to the cause at hand, but also showing the same zeal and love for the masses.

Before I could conclude, a thought struck me. She had said she would consider me as her son henceforth. That meant I should consider

A.Z. Phizo as my would-be brother. I wondered how I should deal with him if I were confronted by him. My disciplined mind replied, "Deal with him according to the regulations of law and order. The law respects none. In the eyes of God and the law of the country, everyone is treated equally, big or small, kith or kin."

13

HUMAN NATURE IS THE SAME

I was out on a mission to meet an important hostile leader. His emissary, who had very high ideas about him, came to meet me. Instead of speaking about business, he started blasting me on various subjects. I had come across many characters, including some senior officers, who started conversations with vocal bombardment to impress their personalities on others. The most important subjects he mentioned were:

a. The hostile Nagas had sent many of their representatives to foreign countries and were sure of returning with independence. Hence, I should not undermine the authority of the hostile Naga Federal Authority whom he was representing.

b. He wanted to know why, from his experience during World War II when he was a boy and British, American, and Japanese troops came to Naga Hills, the forces ran after the girls! Had they no families? Had they no sisters and wives?

In response to his first question, I asked him whether independence was a commodity that could be purchased outside one's own country and carried back in a haversack to be planted on the mother soil or could be donated by someone. He replied that this secret was best known to their leaders only. I gave him the names of the hostile Nagas, including A.Z. Phizo, who had gone to Burma and Pakistan. In the former country, they were under arrest, and in Pakistan, they were secretly living as guests. I told him frankly that the day Phizo left Nagaland in quest of independence, they had lost the fight.

Referring to his second point, I told him that the cause of his complaint remained universal. Even if the troops were not there, the flirtation would continue in one form or another if the desire on the part of the opposite sex was there. I drew his attention to the conditions prevailing in Naga Hills where women outnumbered men 2 to one, and where divorced women had the freedom to lead a free life. I also drew his attention to the various instructions issued by the Naga National Council on the subject. The Naga National Council, the respective Tribal Councils, The Naga Youth Movement organization, and the Naga Women's Federation had time and again issued letters to the locals as well as to the women not to be intimate with non-Nagas. In some cases, they imposed fines and punishments and finally established the check posts leading from the Naga Hills to the plains to ensure that no more than one woman should accompany each Naga male proceeding to markets in the plains. Still, the problem remained unsolved.

Having heard me, he replied, "What you say is true, but why can't the troops, who are the guardians of law, order, and security of one's own country, teach the girls who are trying to go astray to behave properly and stay at home?"

I did not reply, for I had concluded that any further discussion would not be fruitful. But he mistook my silence and, to recover the lost ground, he restarted his vocal bombardment again. I did not interrupt but lit cigarettes, one after another, until he stopped and requested one. When I lit his cigarette, he asked, "What have you to say?"

I just smiled and placed a drink in front of him, telling him, "Drink it. Your throat must be dry after all the steam you have blown off." He looked at me curiously and, after lifting the glass, turned it bottoms up.

Placing the glass on the table, he said, "Can I have another one?" He had 2 quick ones and then asked, "What's next?"

I instructed my orderly to take the visitor with him. Then turning to the guest, I said, "You must be hungry. Go and have your lunch. We will continue our discussion afterward."

Without uttering a word, he left. After his lunch, we talked business. I gave my message to his boss and got up. "I think it is time we should part. You will require some time before dusk to return to your jungle hideout. Every one of the security forces in the area has orders to ensure that you return safely and unobstructed."

I clasped the man's hand firmly as we bid each other farewell. Suddenly, he turned back and spoke in a pleading tone, "May I make a humble request of you, kind sir?"

I replied, "Of course, what is it?"

"Could you please permit my wife and me to spend the night in our humble abode here in the village? We hail from this place, and I promise to leave early in the morning," he implored, pointing toward his home where his wife stood waiting.

"When was the last time you were here?" I inquired. "About a month ago, sir. I sneaked in during the night and left before dawn," he confessed.

Without hesitation, I granted his request, much to his delight. I approached the Post commander, a jolly old Gorkha Subedar, and informed him of the man's request. The Subedar chuckled and replied, "Certainly, Sir. Let him stay. At least one of our women will have one less man to worry about for the next few days!"

As the man strode away, his heart singing with joy, he suddenly turned back and called out to me, "Could you do me one more favor, Sir?"

"Of course, what do you need?" I responded.

"Could you spare me at least half a bottle of rum? I have been coming home secretly, never comfortable in my own home for fear of arrest. But with your assurance, I can finally relax and enjoy a carefree evening with my beloved wife," he requested earnestly.

Without a second thought, I granted his wish, and he went on his way, his humble abode not far from where I was stationed. As the night wore on, I could hear singing and merriment emanating from his home.

The next morning, the man returned to bid me farewell with a beaming smile on his face. He saluted me smartly and exclaimed, "Sir, I must thank you from the bottom of my heart! For the first time in 2 years, I had a carefree and happy night. You have earned my respect and admiration!"

I must beg for forgiveness for my reprehensible behavior yesterday. If only others possessed the same tolerance and kindness as you, misunderstandings could be avoided. The movement should be called off as soon as possible."

As he was leaving, I spoke up. "Yesterday, you left my question about the behavior of troops unanswered. You are a high-ranking hostile leader, or at least you claim to be. Yet, the desire to spend the night with your wife led you to beg not only for permission to stay in the village but also for a bottle of rum. I do not blame you for your human tendencies, and I appreciate your honesty. But what about the security forces? They leave their families for years at a time to ensure your safety and prosperity. They, too, possess the same human tendencies as you. Do you truly believe that if a woman neither initiates nor tolerates advances, anyone would behave otherwise?"

He started laughing and said, "I am sorry for what I said yesterday. Staying in the jungle makes one think in a one-sided way. Moreover, having joined the hostile camp, we have developed the habit of criticizing everything about the government to impress our people. I will never complain again on that point. Our Naga youths behave the same way, and our Naga Home Guards are not an exception."

Sometime later, he came to meet me in Kohima with a reply. Handing over the letter, he said, "This is the last errand I will undertake for the hostiles. I am tired of living in the jungle. Our leaders are not true to their words. Please arrange for my surrender."

It was not a difficult task.

14

A SENSE OF PROPORTION IS A MUST AT ALL TIMES

The select committee of the Naga People's Convention was due to meet at Mokokchung, and everyone was preparing to go. Several representatives who had gathered from the adjoining areas had dropped in at my office for a conference. They were taken back to their respective places after dusk. I was sitting at my desk, writing up notes for the day when there was a knock on the door. I opened it and saw uniformed men standing there. Immediately, I knew that they were not members of the Indian Armed Forces but were hostile Nagas. One of them spoke, "Sir, can we come in? We want to talk with you."

I had expected them to force their way in, and as such, I was surprised at their polite request. For a moment, I hesitated but then asked them to come in. Their faces beamed with delight when I offered them cigarettes and drinks. "We would love to have them. It has been a year since we have tasted such things. The last occasion was a free issue of rum, beer, milk tins, and butter which we got due to a wrong airdrop," their leader said.

They then introduced themselves. One was a Brigadier, 2 Lieutenant Colonels, and 2 Majors of the so-called Naga Home Guard organization of the hostiles. One of the Majors, a Rengma Naga, had recently received training in a foreign country in demolition and sabotage. They had brought a letter from their General. It was a short one.

"Dear Respected Father,

Five of my officers who wish to ascertain, on my behalf, the real intention of the meeting to be held at Mokokchung, are being sent by me to meet you."

The difference between these 5 and other hostile Nagas was that the former lived with the delegates and had ample opportunities to discuss things with them freely. They also came to meet me on 2 occasions. After their return to Kohima, they journeyed into the jungle to report to their General. A few days later, they returned to Kohima and surrendered to lead a peaceful life. At the subsequent meeting, I tried to find out the reasons behind the psychological change in them. I could only conclude that frankness and kindness from everyone had made them change their views.

The murder of Shri Satsuo Angami created a tense situation in Kohima. The culprits had been arrested. Hence, I went to Shillong to discuss the situation with Shri S.M. Dutt and the Governor of Assam. Despite the differences with Angami, on many counts, one and all felt upset over his murder. The need for vengeance, Renne, head for head, was taking deep roots in the minds of Satsuo's supporters, and they started clamoring that Phizo's wife and children, who were staying in Shillong, be forced to return to Naga Hills so that revenge could be taken. I had alerted the authorities at Shillong regarding the talk of revenge and the measures that were taken to ensure that no untoward incident occurred.

I needed a break and decided to take some time off to spend with my family and look into household affairs. To my surprise, the eldest daughter of A.Z. Phizo, accompanied by her brother, came to my house to meet me. I had met them earlier at Ghanpari after their surrender to the government. My wife and children were also surprised and cautioned me not to spend hours talking, as I had promised to take them out.

The daughter of Phizo asked for my reaction to finding them in my house. I told them frankly I was surprised and then requested them to state the reason for their visit. They were contemplating proceeding to Kohima and asked me whether they could go. I told them that they were free to go anywhere and there were no restrictions on their movements, and as such, I could not understand why they should ever ask me the question.

After a pause, they came out with the real intention of the visit. They wanted travel facilities, an escort, and above all, protection from an armed guard during their stay at Kohima. I brought to their notice the possible difficulties of such a procedure and that it was unlikely that the government would agree to undertake responsibility for their safety during the journey and at Kohima.

I also cautioned them about the atmosphere prevailing in Kohima after the murder of Satsuo Angami and suggested that it would be in their interest to defer going to Kohima for some more months.

It appeared that they did not appreciate the suggestion and were irritated. In anger, they accused me of trying to prevent them from going to Nagaland where they had the right to stay and emphasized that they must go.

Unable to understand their attitude, I got up to end the meeting and told them to either approach the administration for all the arrangements they desired for their security or to go on their own. They promptly replied that they were aware that they would not get any help from the administration as they were not proceeding on official duty and hence had come to me.

I told them that I had no forces at my command to provide them with an escort except the goodwill of the people and once again advised them not to go to Kohima for the time being. In the end, I drew their attention to the situation and the danger to their own lives. They did not appreciate my words and left me in an angry mood without even wishing me a good day.

After nearly 6 months, I was in Shillong. Miss Beliou Angami came to my place with the daughter and son of A.Z. Phizo. She said, "I brought them intentionally. I know they were angry when you advised them not to go to Kohima. But it is a good thing you did. They have realized it. They will thank you individually, but I must appreciate that you can be good to the people who are considered enemies by others."

I told her that as far as children were concerned, they should not be blamed for the deeds of their parents and should be allowed to lead a life and career toward prosperity unblemished. Among the children, none could be called an enemy. All were friends and deserved goodwill and affection, and if this was done, at least the next generation would learn to live with love and affection instead of crossing swords. While I was speaking, I recollected another incident in Kohima. One of the most notorious individuals from Kohima village had joined the hostiles and accepted the post of "Ranu Peyu" in the hostile organization. In due time, his family also joined him in the jungle as they could live a more comfortable life there on the loot collected from Kohima village and Kheti huts. The individual committed innumerable atrocities on the villagers of Kohima and even killed some. As the security forces, who had so far stayed concentrated, started fanning out, the family found life in the jungle miserable, and along with their father and mother who had also joined the hostiles, they had to shift their abode every day. The individual quietly sent his children back to the Kohima village one by one.

It caused a commotion in Kohima. The aggrieved persons wanted to take revenge by killing them. Someone brought them to my office for safety. After a great effort, I persuaded Satsuo and the 4 Gaon Buras to undertake responsibility for their safety and told them that as families of most of the hostile Nagas lived undisturbed in the respective villages, these children should be given the same privilege. Turning to Beliou, I said, "Whether I am right or not, one thing is certain: the children of Phizo have no place in Naga Hills at present if they wish to live safely and peacefully. These conditions will prevail until such time that either the customary laws are changed, or the memories of the atrocities committed by the hostile Nagas fade. Probably Phizo's family is the only one who has suffered this fate." The raid on Kohima and the cutting off communications from all sides had caused innumerable problems for everyone. The important Gaon Buras and leaders from Kohima were kidnapped by the hostile Nagas. The people who had dispersed all over were more worried about their kith and kin who had remained untraceable and the property they had left behind in the village. It was difficult to have even one meal a day as the stocks left behind in the village were inaccessible to them.

15

BUILDING A SUSTAINABLE RAPPORT WITH PEOPLE

The administration was also confronted with a herculean task. The Deputy Commissioner, a very courageous and magnificent man, was faced with problems all over the Naga Hills, which he had to deal with single-handedly. Unfortunately, the other officers did not enjoy much confidence from the people. In addition to the problems of the administration and the needs of the people of Kohima, he had to cope with the needs of the armed forces.

He came to my office and requested help in getting men to work as porters for the security forces, especially as none were in the mood to come forward to work, afraid to go out. I was rather surprised at his request and wondered whether I could do it. I suggested that he could get other officers under him to do the job, but he told me, "No one else but you can influence the people at this moment. They may not even listen to me for lack of security accorded, which is not my fault. They have temporarily lost faith in me also. The commander of the security forces is pressing me continuously and warning me that if porters are not available, they will not move an inch, irrespective of the consequences. The regular porters are also not tractable."

As I had the greatest regard for the Deputy Commissioner and taking into consideration the needs of the security forces, I went to the town and got hold of Satsuo, Vikrulle, and a few other Nagas who had a good following. Standing over a vehicle, I requested men, women, and children to come forward. The people were in a disturbed state of mind, but to my surprise, 2 hundred men, women, and children came forward. They said that they would work and do anything at my bidding, provided in the evening I got a meal for them. Without taking into consideration how I would do it, I promised them, and they went on to perform the errands given.

Once they joined, I devoted myself to fulfilling my promise of procuring food for them with the help of security forces, women, and children. Rice and other requirements were brought to the town to feed them.

For the next 7 days, I had to undertake the same task, and it was carried out. The result was that my office became the main center of liaison. Though overworked, I had one great satisfaction: that in the hour of need, I could do my additional bit for the administration and the security forces who were there to safeguard the interest of the nation. Also, the fact that even in difficult times I could influence the Nagas, not directly but through their own acknowledged elders of position, gave me a new line of thought, and I decided to make use of it to advance the national cause. The important points I learned and noted were that the people liked frankness and that the promise given must be kept.

The surrender of underground political workers and the hostiles confronted the Government with a new problem of rehabilitating them. Many of them were unwilling to return to their earlier profession of cultivation. The educated youths clamored for scholarships to continue their education in places like Shillong, Delhi, Bombay, and Calcutta.

One of the Tatars (Members of the Parliament) of the so-called Naga Federal Authority from the Ao area, an elderly but uneducated person who surrendered, had come to Kohima in search of a job and was guided to my office by one of his friends. When he explained the purpose of his visit, I was wondering how I could help and what type of job I could suggest to an ex-member of Parliament. Ultimately, I asked him, "What is your ambition? What do you expect?" He replied that he would be happy if he could get a job as a Sardar (headman) of labor gangs working on roads.

I phoned the Deputy Commissioner, who obliged by giving an immediate appointment to the man as a Sardar of 10 porters. The unsettled economic conditions, coupled with the creation of new posts in the chain of administration, had brought about a craze among job hunters. Not only those who had graduated but also those who had learned to wear a suit and tie and could afford to purchase one were going around in circles aspiring to secure a job. Job hunters were rushing to Shillong to get new suits stitched so they could impress the authorities.

This not only started jealousies, hatred, and false reporting against each other but also caused great worry to the elders, who even today are pillars of society in the Naga Hills. I was also perturbed by the queue outside my office of these job seekers and the time spent listening to their self-praise and grievances. One and all advanced the common argument that either they had been loyal to the Government and suffered at the hands of the hostiles due to their loyalty, or they should have a preference as they had abandoned underground activities and as such, it was the responsibility of the Government to provide them with suitable means to promote an equal position to the one they held when underground. Tribes other than Aos and Angamis maintained that individuals from their tribes, being uneducated, had not received fair representation in the Government service so far and as such they should have a preference, although they were less educated compared to Aos and Angamis.

Irrespective of the fact that I could only recommend them and had no authority to appoint them, my office continued to be flooded with applications that the individuals brought personally. The main reason for their coming to my office, irrespective of the result, was that they had a patient hearing.

16

EDUCATED, YOUNG, AND SEEKING GOVERNMENT JOBS

On one occasion, elders accompanied by Visar Angami came to my office. During the talk, subjects like education, the evil effects of the disturbances on society, and rivalry among job seekers and its effect on the elders came up for discussion. One of the very elderly and influential Gaon Buras spoke bitterly, "It used to be that age and experience received the highest respect in Naga Hills. But times have changed. Sweet talk, best-tailored clothes, and a certificate either from a college or school are the ones that count for securing a position. At a cost to society and the Government, they gain experience by experimenting. Take the example of the circle officer appointed in our area. Though graduated, he used to seek my advice and never disobeyed any of the orders I gave to my Khel and the village. Now he stays in the town, comes at 10 o'clock in his jeep, dressed in a suit and with all pomp and show, and sends for me to meet him in the office he has established in a newly built hut!"

Having paused a moment and glanced at the others, he continued, "I have to wait for hours outside before I am called in. If I say anything against what he is proposing, he shouts at me, "You are uneducated. The world is changing, developing, and progressing. This is the age of nuclear weapons and revolutionized thoughts." "Well, I must obey him and say 'yes' to anything he desires, however wrong it may be."

"Once the youths see that I am humiliated - ones who sat at my feet a few days earlier - how can they respect me? When they see that my advice is not heeded, how can they obey me or my other elderly colleagues? I always had a direct approach to the Deputy Commissioner, but now when I go to him, he asks whether I have seen the circle officer. If I say yes, D.C. says that I will get a decision through the circle officer. If I represent the case to the circle officer, he is unable to give a decision and says that he must get orders from the Deputy Commissioner. Previously, in one visit, we solved our problems and returned with firm orders, but now we must go in circles and wait and wait. With the new era, the youth feel that we, the elders, have become like rusted swords and they are the atom and hydrogen bombs. It could be the case, but the trouble is that every youth feels that individually, he is better and superior to the one appointed by the Government, and thus they do not see eye to eye, resulting in disorder and disobedience."

"True, very true!" another Gaon Bura shouted, "And for that, the Government blames us for the disorder and disobedience. Time and again, we are warned that we are losing hold over the villagers, and we must tighten our grip. It is the irony of fate that we are treated so! If we had discarded our red cloth in the days when the disturbances were at their peak, the administrative machinery would have disintegrated and melted, to become inoperative. But we were oath-bound. Despite the pressure from the hostiles and though we were at their mercy and without protection, we kept the administrative machinery working."

An elderly Gaon Bura, equally influential and important, with gray hair and better literary qualifications, shouted, "The disturbances have already brought about changes in the economic and social structure of the Nagas, disintegrating the well-knit society. If these continue and develop, I am sure in due time Naga Hills will be faced with a situation common to others but unheard of among Nagas: acute problems of political strife, communism, and trade unions. God save us from that catastrophe."

Wrapping the red blanket properly over his body and lighting the cigarette that I had offered him earlier, he said, "At Dimapur, one of the young officers from other parts of India was telling me that at the high level in the Indian National Congress organization, the gray-haired leaders would not allow the youths to come anywhere near them and were keeping their grip over power. As a result of this, there was a continuous struggle between youth and age in the Congress organization. He also told me that though the youths have failed to capture power in Congress, they have outclassed the aged in the administration and captured the executive power, leaving the temporary posts of governors and ministers for the aged. Is it true?

"It must be true," one of the Gaon Buras roared. "It must be true. Since the British left, we have not seen a single gray-haired administrator coming to Naga Hills. All who came were young men. They come and go before they know us. I was attending a party given by our circle officer to the army and civil officers. When I asked him why he spent so much money on parties, he said that now in every service, social contact and entertainment are valued more than professional ability and efficiency for promotion and progress." Turning to me, he asked, "Tell us why it is so!"

I was relieved from the task of answering by Visar Angami, who was still calm. He spoke in a gentle voice. "I think we have missed the main point, and we are drifting off course as our passions are aroused by our sentiments. The main defect lies in the system of imparting education. Many other parts of India have already tasted the fruits of it. The system of education introduced by the British and the missionaries neither suits Naga Hills nor any other part of India."

He continued, "From the day a child enters school, he is unwillingly made to part from the Earth. He is taught to think that manual labor is below dignity, and he loses touch with nature and its importance. Within the 4 walls of the classroom, he is made to cram all the books into memory. Students learn subjects like Botany and nature study within those 4 walls. Our colonel's son knows all about a frog and a reptile but has not seen one. The students are taught to join processions for one reason or another, are made to arrange receptions and sing songs in praise of Tom, Dick, and Harry who visit the school in one capacity or the other to get a donation for the school and are made to believe that such acts can deliver the desired goods to them.

"They are taught the history of emperors, fighters, and conquerors, but nothing about the farmer or common man who can use his land best and deliver the goods for the betterment and livelihood of human beings. In these schools, they learn to earn money by all other means except manual labor as if it is a sin to dirty one's hands with the good Earth. Our schools are turning out 'Sahibs' and 'Memsahibs.'"

"The system of education must be revolutionized. A youth of today knows all about Julius Caesar, Edward VIII, Pat Boone, Lata Mangeshkar, Nargis, Raj Kapoor, the atom bomb, and jetliners, but is not able to recount the name of his grandfather, what he did, the customary laws of his country, or who founded his village, why a particular name was given to his village and the history of his family. If we want to save Naga Hills from ruin and disaster resulting from isms, we will have to prevail upon the government that agriculture and the use of natural resources for a livelihood be given primary importance and taught simultaneously with the alphabet and tables. If we do not do so, we will perish."

The discussion and airing of views would probably have carried on for some time, but just then the constable on duty came in to inform me that youths with representation for service had been waiting for a long time and wanted to meet me urgently. Visar shouted, "Age and youth have a common consolation in this office," then got up to leave.

The craze for making new suits had reached a climax! With the best-tailored suits, it appeared that those who wore them equally needed financial help. To my surprise, one day, a postman turned up with 2 V.P.P. parcels amounting to rupees 700. These were addressed in my name by a well-known tailoring firm in Shillong. I declined to take delivery.

A month later, a messenger delivered a letter from 2 hostile leaders who had previously gone to Shillong to meet the Governor of Assam. They were inquiring about a parcel of 4 suits they had ordered and wanted to know if it had been received. They wanted me to hand them over to their messenger. I explained to the messenger what had happened with the tailoring firm's V.P.P. parcels and declined to hand over the suits.

Stipends for higher education in Shillong were being granted liberally to Naga youths. However, many of the stipend recipients, as well as other students, were complaining of a shortage of funds while studying in Shillong. They had built up arrears of fees and boarding charges in schools, and their parents were being continuously pressured for more funds by the students. I worked out the expenditures with the parents, but we could not understand the need for additional amounts. However, one consolation was that the female students never asked for extra pocket money.

During the mid-term break, many students returned to the Naga Hills, and I took this opportunity to investigate the cause of additional expenditures. They all complained of a shortage of funds, despite my calculations showing that the stipends and money provided by their parents were sufficient to cover boarding, lodging, tuition fees, and books, with a small amount left as pocket money. However, they complained of other expenses which were more costly.

As I questioned them further, they explained the cause of the additional expenditure. Their spokesperson said, "Sir, clothes and entertainment are the costliest items. We must have 3 to 4 new suits every year. Furthermore, the girls from our area who are attending school in Shillong expect us to take them out for pictures and picnics on holidays and weekends. It costs more than boarding, lodging, and tuition fees."

I tried to advise them not to be extravagant and to concentrate on studies and simple living, but their spokesperson replied, "What you say is true, but if we do not take these girls out, it will be a shame for us Nagas that girls from our state go out with others because we cannot afford to do so. In Shillong, the students dress properly on holidays and never go by bus but by taxi, and never sit in cinema houses in any other class but the highest. We cannot remain behind."

It was a matter of prestige. I told them to seek the right advice and help of their parents, as the government was unlikely to cater to these needs. After they left, I thought about the problem. They were getting into the habit of spending more than they could earn initially working in any government service! Furthermore, not all of them were likely to get a government job, so the result would be that a new class of disgruntled and disappointed men would spring up. One could only wonder what they would do under such circumstances.

17

A REBEL WHO QUOTES MAHATMA GANDHI!

Visar Angami was a constant source of amusement for one and all. He was the second President of the Naga National Council, an organization formed for the welfare of the Nagas and to unite the fourteen tribes under one banner. In the next contest for the post, he lost by one vote to A. Z. Phizo, and thereafter, the council assumed the role of a political organization.

Most of the time, Visar carried the book Experiments with Truth by Mahatma Gandhi and quoted passages from it to support his arguments. He was one of the few Nagas who had participated in the civil non-cooperation movement launched by Mahatma Gandhi during the pre-Independence period and had courted arrest. Despite his belief in the teachings of Mahatma Gandhi and his ideals, he drank like a fish. He felt very proud and happy when he received a set of books on Mahatma's life as a present from Indira Gandhi after she visited the Naga Hills.

One of the top-ranking officers from Delhi was visiting the Naga Hills. Visar was also introduced to the visitors during the introduction of local leaders and elders. Before the collector could complete the introduction, Visar said, "Sir, once I was the President of N.N.C. Now, I am the self-styled commander-in-chief of N.M.C." A mischievous smile was visible on his face. The visitor appeared puzzled upon hearing this and politely inquired, "I understand that N.N.C. stands for Naga National Council. But I do not know what N.M.C. stands for." Visar replied, "N.M.C. stands for Never Mind Company."

"I meet everyone, small or big, have meals with officials and non-officials, children and elders, underground hostiles, overground friends who either profess loyalty to the government or the hostile Nagas, and everyone else. Everyone, including you, should follow my example. It is the only way to solve the present disturbances, bring about emotional integration between Nagas and the rest of the citizens of India, and restore harmony and peace. When I am not drunk, I weep to see the miseries of my people and sympathize with them. When I am drunk, I laugh and abuse those who started the process to achieve power. You are meeting here with a selected group of people. Come with me to the villages and jungle. You will meet people of all shades of opinion and vision. I will prove that I am correct in advising you what to do." He was seen opening the book Experiments with Truth, as the collector took the visitor to the next elder for introduction.

During the 2nd sitting of the Naga Peoples' Convention in Mokokchung, Visar Angami showed up in a peculiar costume. He was dressed in striped trousers representing the United Kingdom, an American jacket, a Japanese helmet, and bottles of all the famous wines in Europe. He also had a Burmese Lungi tied around his waist. When someone asked him about his unusual attire, he replied, "Haven't you heard about the hostile Naga newsletters emphasizing that they sent representatives to all foreign countries and the United Nations Organization? These delegates returned with assurances of material and help. I am one of those."

The trousers Macmillan was wearing at 10 Downing Street heard my representation of the Naga Case, and he took them off and gave them to me with all his blessings. After my talk with Eisenhower, he immediately presented me with the jacket he wore when he ran after the last German soldier during World War II. The Emperor of Japan was inspired by my talk and presented me with the helmet he was wearing and blessed me with the words, 'Let the rising sunrise regularly and brighter and brighter in your hills every day.' Here are the shoes Keo Tea Fung, Chairman of the Chinese People's Republic, gave me. He said that he had used them for fifteen years during his retreat to the mountains until he dethroned Generalissimo Chiang Kai-shek. The shoes are too big for me and torn, making me look like Charlie Chaplin, who always reminds me of a comic. The soles prick me, but I wear them as a gift from the honored Chairman.

"Here is the Vodka the Prime Minister of Russia gave me," he opened a bottle and sipped the contents. "He told me that if we agreed to consider Russia as a mother country and work as dictated by the Kremlin, they would construct a pipeline from Russia to Naga Hills so that the vodka from the Communist shrine would flow day and night for the use of the Nagas. Look at the Champagne the President of the French Republic gave me. He told me to start nightclubs and open the bottle there. This is the Port from the President of Spain. He said that it was the foundation of the fifth Column. When I went to Burma, the Prime Minister gave me the lungi and told me to become a Bhiku first instead of wasting my time on such errands." Thereupon, Angami opened another bottle and drank half of it.

One of Visar's companions asked him, "Did you go to receive all these things required for independence, arms, or ammunition?" "Of course, as deputed and directed, I went to get the arms, ammunition, and independence."

All countries sympathized with our cause and gave their moral support. But what could you expect from others? Independence is not bought or brought from outside. It must be gained at home. Mahatma Gandhi and Nehru started the independence movement and stayed with the people suffering imprisonment. Like Phizo, they did not run away to Pakistan and the United Kingdom for protection and to live in peace and luxury, leaving the people to suffer.

All the leaders of foreign countries told me that these days the technique of the Cold War, combined with the threat of nuclear weapons, is the practice. Arms and ammunition, therefore, cannot be openly supplied from outside. Hence, we should plead and get it from the Indian Army to fight against the same army if and when the technique of a shooting war is advocated."

After the drinking party, laughter filled the air. Visar slept at the same spot until the morning, only to find that all his rum bottles with labels of foreign liquor were empty. The next day, he was confronted by a few hostile Nagas who threatened and questioned him about his insolent talk regarding them. Visar gaily replied, "If you want to prove me wrong, then the one who has been to a foreign country and brought the help as stated by you can come forward!"

18

LESSONS ON SURVIVAL

Surendra Mohan Kar, who had gone out for his usual morning round, returned hurriedly with his Naga friend and came straight to Visar's breakfast table. "I want to attend a meeting some leaders are having with the Naga hostiles," he said. "Can I take the jeep?" Having ascertained the details, Visar gave his consent and wished him good luck. But as the vehicle was about to leave, I stopped it. I ran to my room and returned with a bottle of rum. Thrusting it into his hands, I said, "Take it, you may find it useful."

It was getting dark, but Kar had not yet returned. Consequently, I was feeling anxious. Even though, by our conduct, behavior, and sympathetic attitude, my staff and I had earned goodwill among the Nagas, including hostiles. Still, 4 of them had been killed by the hostile Nagas. I took many risks, but when it was the turn of my subordinates, I hesitated, and in the event, they were out on such errands, I always felt anxious and worried about their safety till they returned. I phoned the security force near the place Kar had gone. They confirmed that the jeep was parked near the post and the driver was sitting in the camp, yet Kar and his companion had not returned from the jungle. The news caused me more worry, and I was unable to concentrate on my work. I decided that if Kar did not return within half an hour, I would personally go to help him in case he was in difficulty. Just then, the telephone buzzed to convey the news that Kar had reached the post of the security forces and had left for Kohima.

The news relieved me, and I settled down to work at the desk. After about fifteen minutes, Kar walked into my office. He was excited. As usual, he rubbed his fingers over his mustache. Before I could ask him to sit, he said, "I cannot express my gratitude to you. But for the bottle of rum you gave me, I would have lost my life." Signaling him to sit down, I said, "I was worried about your safety. I take risks, but in the future, I will not allow you to undertake such missions. Tell us what happened?"

"Well," he said, "Our meeting started well. There were 40 hostiles, all armed. My friends had a frank discussion with them. I also took part in it. When we had come to an understanding, one of the hard-core hostiles, who designated himself as a Captain, walked in late in the evening with a pistol in hand. He came straight to me shouting, 'You belong to the Intelligence Department of the Government of India. Why have you come here? You will not go back alive.' Saying so, he pressed the revolver against my ribs."

He paused for a minute. "My hair stood up with fright. I was about to lose my temper, which I controlled somehow. My friends tried in vain to remove the revolver. He was adamant. Just then an idea struck me." He paused. Anxious to hear how he saved himself, I asked, "Then what happened? What did you do?"

"I told him to wait a second," wiping sweat from his forehead, Kar went on, "Then I suggested to him that it would be better for us to share the bottle of rum before he killed me, otherwise the bottle might break, and the rum would go to waste. At this, the hostile Captain shouted, 'Don't tell a lie! If you had any rum, you would have shared it with others earlier.' "Believe me that I have a bottle of rum, and as I was told that you would be coming here, I thought we might wait till your arrival." Saying so, I gently pushed his revolver aside and, taking out the bottle of rum from my pocket, I placed it on the table. His face brightened up.

Throwing his revolver on the ground, he grasped the bottle and said that he was glad that I had spoken the truth. My friend quietly removed the captain's pistol a few feet away. When the Captain had 2 quick ones, I got up and asked him to excuse me as I wanted to ease myself."

"He shouted that I must return, as he had to settle many accounts with me. When I came out, the wife of the host whispered to me to accompany her. When we were out of hearing distance, she told me that her husband had signaled her to lead me safely to the post of the security forces and that my friend would follow. This so-called hostile captain is a bloodthirsty man. His kith and kin do not trust him," Kar said as he took the cup of tea I had ordered. "She guided me to the road. My friend joined me. He was escorted by the host,"

"I congratulate you for your presence of mind," I said as I patted him on the back. "Well, Sir, Almighty God saved me," Kar replied, getting up and folding his hands. "Probably you also know what is best for us. The bottle of rum you gave me, plus the moment, plus the thirst for liquor of the people of the land, helped to save my life."

One day, when the pressure of work in my office was less, I decided to visit some of the villages in the Southern Angami Area without prior notice. As soon as I arrived at Kigwema village, I learned that, with the due knowledge and permission of the concerned authorities, the villagers were having discussions with 3 hundred armed hostiles in Vishwema and Jakhama. The village defense guards warned me not to proceed further since I only had an unarmed driver with me.

To avoid any suspicion, I went up to Mao village on the border of Naga Hills and Manipur State and then visited Khuzama village. There, one of my old friends, Sapro Angami, and the village elders informed me about the presence of hostiles in the 2 villages and hoped that some fruitful outcome would result from the talk. They cautioned me that, in my interest, I should not visit any of the villages, as some of the hostile Nagas were hot-tempered. The more the villagers told me not to go to these places, the more determined I was to visit. As I approached Viswema, I saw a sentry in plain clothes standing there. When I had passed Viswema earlier, he had not been there. He wore a Naga shawl. As I parked my car at the entrance of the village, a few Gaon Buras, followed by one of the leaders of the Naga People's Convention, came over. They traditionally received me but showed no sign of taking me inside the village.

We talked about general subjects, and then, to their greatest surprise, I directly opened the subject of the meeting that was being held in the village and the presence of the hostile Nagas. Finding no alternative, they discussed it in a reserved manner. Determined as I was to move into the village, I inquired about the welfare of the wife of a friend of mine who had been ailing for some time, and then I expressed a desire to meet her and inquire personally.

All of them started gazing at each other without answering me. As none moved, I got hold of the hand of John Angami and pulled him toward his house. Two elderly Gaon Buras rushed forward and then kept pace a few steps ahead of me. I realized that they were acting as guards for me. Also, I was fully aware of the embarrassing and difficult situation they were facing. I could see the eyes peeping at me from doors and windows. At places, I saw rifle muzzles pointing. Children who were accustomed to meeting me also came forward with a greeting.

Having visited the house of my friend and inquired about his wife, I made my way to John's house. We sat there for half an hour and had the customary Madhu (rice beer). I casually asked John about the names of the big shots among the hostiles in the village and their mood and then left. At the entrance of the village, I apologized to them for the difficult situation created by me and wished them success in their mission.

Then, I went to Jakhama village. I parked the jeep at a safe distance in the vicinity of the post manned by the security forces and walked to the village. One of the elders met me at the entrance, taken by surprise at my coming on that day and at that time. I asked him to accompany me to the house of Visar Angami, which was in the heart of the village. Walking along the narrow paths in the village, I could see that even the children showed surprise at my presence. Intentionally, I talked loudly with the elder while walking.

As we approached Visar's house, the elder shouted, and Visar came out hurriedly. "My God, how did you walk in? Today is not a good day to visit the village. The weather is misty, though the sun is shining. The paths are muddy, and we have Genna. No one has either entered or left the village. My house is full of my wife's relatives. Let us go and sit in my friend's house." With the usual smile and mischievous eyes, he spoke loudly.

As we walked to his friend's house, I whispered, "How many in your house?" "Sixteen," he whispered back, "including a General. All are armed. But I do not know whether they have ammunition!" Saying so, he laughed loudly and walked ahead to his friend's house. But he returned without going in. "It is too dirty inside. Ten in all."

I started laughing at his gestures. I told him that I had not come to sit and drink Madhu, but just wanted to inquire how the people were doing; hence, he should not worry about finding a clean and suitable place for me to sit. I told him loudly so that others could hear that I had heard of the presence of hostiles in the village for a meeting. However, I felt that I had an equal right and freedom to move through the village, so I had come. We walked through the village, cutting jokes and inquiring about the welfare of those I knew. Then, we returned to the village perimeter. All the Gaon Buras joined us while walking in the village. I now told them to return to their guests and thanked them. When I came near the jeep, one of the officers of the security forces who was standing near an adjacent tree came running forward. "Thank God you have returned safely. Our sentry spotted the jeep. At first, we thought it was that of the circle officer, but soon we realized it was your vehicle. The news that you had gone alone to the village caused us great anxiety. We have instructions not to go anywhere near the village until tomorrow morning. We have kept a strong patrol ready in case anything happens."

I thanked him for all his kind thoughts and precautions taken. Meanwhile, his commanding officer, who was a great friend of mine, walked up. Shaking hands, he said, "Well done. Everyone appears to be so worried about you going to the village. I told them that you would not be harmed by anyone, yet I kept a patrol ready as ordered by the higher headquarters." I went to their mess and had tea. Everyone was eager to know what was happening in the village. One of the young officers apologetically asked, "If it was not your intention to meet the hostiles, then what was the purpose of your visit to the village?" "To test the faith, sincerity, and power of locals who have not joined the hostile camp. Furthermore, why should we ban ourselves from visiting the village just because hostile Nagas are there? It would be conceding privileges to others. I also wanted to test my courage."

The next day, I received a note from the hostile Naga General. It read, "I admire your courage and sincerity. But for the pressure of the locals, many of us would have liked to talk to you across the table."

19

SIMPLE QUESTIONS BUT TRICKY SITUATIONS

The disappointment, frustration, and helplessness caused in the minds of Ngully and his widowed aged mother over the loss of one thousand rupees were worth all the sympathy one could have. Their friends sympathized but were unable to assist them. It was not a case of robbery, loss, or theft. The promise to pay was there, but it had ceased to be a legal tender.

Ngully was educated, but his father was not. A simple but intelligent man of courage and devotion, he worked throughout his life to earn his bread and to save a little for his children who were yet teenagers at the time of his death. During World War II, he assisted the Allied forces and was amply rewarded for it in cash. He died early, leaving the kids to the care of their mother. Unnerved, she worked in the fields, at home, and sent the children to school for education.

Ngully was a brilliant student with exceptional ability. He took a keen interest in the day-to-day developments in Naga Hills but refused to be drawn blindly into it. Instead, he devoted himself to the study of the causes of the unrest, the history, and held discussions with leaders of all shades of thought. When the disturbances started in Naga Hills, he toured the Lotha area extensively at the risk of his life, persuading the people to avoid violence and trying his best to educate them regarding the constitutional means of achieving anything. He also worked voluntarily as a link between the Security Forces and the people.

His activities were misunderstood by the hostile Nagas, who burned and destroyed his house and other belongings in the village. Fortunately, his aged mother and sister, however, escaped unhurt. The loss was a heavy one, but with his cool temperament, Ngully faced it as inevitable. He evacuated his mother and sister to the town and once again devoted all his energies to the cause at hand.

Once a semblance of normalcy was restored, Ngully was faced with conflicting thoughts. His mother left for the village to rebuild their house and restart cultivation. People urged him to be their representative in the new setup, but his mother and friends advised him to continue his education. Ultimately, Ngully decided to continue his studies, but the question of financial assistance caused a temporary setback. Assisted by his mother and friends, he re-joined school, but often the pressing needs of the people in his area distracted his attention.

Many of the hostile Nagas who surrendered as advised by Ngully received government scholarships and stipends for education, but he was not one of the fortunate lads to receive such financial aid. He was disliked by both the hostiles and the authorities for being out-spoken and refusing to be their man.

He thought for days over the prospects of higher education and was about to give up the idea of joining the college at Shillong and accept a post of teacher when his mother, to whom Ngully was all in all, came to his aid. She advised him to go outside Naga Hills and continue his education undisturbed. She gave him a thousand-rupee note, "This is what your father earned as a reward for bravery and devotion during the war. I had kept it buried from the day he died so that it may be of use to you. I have a few more, but I cannot find them yet. I may succeed in tracing the place where I kept the money, or it may have been burned with the house. This will provide for your expenditure for a year. I will save some more for you by then." Ngully came to Shillong only to be disappointed.

He was told at the State Bank of India that the thousand-rupee note Ngully demanded was illegal tender now. "How can that be? The words 'I promise to pay' and the signature are still there!" He tried in vain at all quarters.

His mother was sorrier and more shocked than he was. She cried when she heard of it. "How could it be illegal tender? Government currency notes are as good as gold and silver. Gold and silver never lose value. I preserved it with great hopes. It is written there that the Government promises to pay, and it has not been canceled!"

When she was told the reasons for making it an illegal tender and of the Government notification which was given wide publicity through the press, Ngully's mother was more puzzled. "But it never reached our ears in the village," she pointed out. "I did not hear of it. It was by hard work that my husband got it. It is a reward for bravery, and the promise to pay must be kept. How can a promise once given be canceled by any notice? We Nagas take an oath and make a promise, and we sacrifice our lives to keep it. We never cancel it by word or notice."

She could not be convinced. She looked with amazement at the rubber stamps put over the note by the bank, declaring it illegal tender, and dropped it on the ground. Thereafter, she refused to touch even a rupee note!

20

LIFE HAS NOT BEEN EASY FOR YOUNG WOMEN

During the raid on Kohima in June 1956, several locals were suspected of fifth-column activities and were detained. The arrested persons included a charming girl but confused.

When she was getting into the police van, someone saw her tearing a sheet of paper and throwing it along the route to the jail, piece by piece. The individual collected the pieces and brought them to me. These were adjusted and pasted together. It turned out to be a photograph of 2 noted Naga personalities taken while studying in a college in Shillong. One had become an officer with status in government service, and the other was a Kilonser (Cabinet Minister) among the hostiles.

There were differences of opinion among the men at the helm in power about how to deal with love and romance among the Nagas. As late as 1958, the screening of full-length films which had any scene of love and romance was not screened in Kohima as it would affect the morale of the Nagas. Yet Nagas visiting Dimapur and other places in the plains of Shillong flooded the cinema houses every night.

I always wondered but never got a correct answer. The eternal desire of women to beautify themselves from head to toe so that they looked attractive, and their burning flame of love and motherhood were inherent in every female, whether born in the most advanced place or the remotest corner. The Naga Hills were no exception. The well-knit society, customs, and traditions provided ample opportunities for the young ones to have love affairs. The 'morang' where girls stayed was a place of attraction for the boys. Fields where they worked together singing and the common meeting places were other avenues for making advances to each other.

However, the systems and customs were different for each tribe. Except among Semes, marrying more than one girl at a time was banned. Semas could have more than one wife, and the rich men had 6 to 7 wives. In one village during the sowing season, the boys and girls are cast in pairs by lottery and until the sowing of all the fields by the girls is over, they are not permitted to live as husband and wife. Rich young men from another village in the same area keep a lookout for a girl who is courted by the largest number of men and then decide their bets (bride price!) since she is liked by so many young men. The competition among wealthy young boys is considerable, and the one offering the largest amount succeeds in getting her as his wife.

Anyway, screening of the individuals arrested during the Kohima raid was essential, and it was undertaken by a team of experts. I gave the pasted together photograph and a pair of scissors to one of the members of the team who knew the charming girl who had ripped up the picture. Before the investigation of the individual began, he showed her the photograph. On seeing it, she blushed and exclaimed, "How did these pieces get together?"

Jokingly, he replied, "Love cannot be easily parted. The pieces came flying to Pandit; he expressed sorrow at your cruelty. He has sent the photograph to you. Would you like to have it?" She smiled and stretched out her hand, saying, "Please give it to me. It is everything to me. I tore it being afraid that I would be searched in jail and unnecessarily my friend would come under suspicion." The investigating officer promptly placed the pair of scissors in her hand and said, "Select the better half."

Once again, she blushed, placing the pair of scissors on the table. She said, "Pandit knows who he is. He knows me perhaps better than I know myself. Why does he tease me? Tell him to keep the photograph with him until I am released."

The photograph was returned to her after her release in the next few days. It has been years since both of the gentlemen in the photograph got married to other girls and became fathers of a few children, but the girl who was arrested remains a spinster!

The Naga People's Convention held at Kohima and the acceptance of the resolutions by the government brought a change in administrative ideas, and new young administrators arrived with enthusiasm, new ideas, and glory. On seeing them, one of the elders remarked, "It appears angels have arrived. Let us hope they will bring us peace and prosperity!"

On hearing this, one of the Naga youths smiled and said, "Whether we get peace and prosperity or not, one thing is sure: that the news will delight the fairies in our land." Soon, the families of the young officers followed them, attired in gowns and scarves. The youths felt happy, but it was rumored that the fairies were very much disappointed. As rules applicable to the members of the security forces were enforced, and Naga Hills was declared a "non-family station" for members of all other services on duty in Naga Hills.

One of the directives issued by Krisanisa Angami, then the President of the so-called Naga Federal Authority, to the girls who had joined the hostile ranks, and the replies given by the girls and boys, gave insight into the minds of the girls and the anxiety of the society.

In the directive, Krisanisa had instructed the girls who had joined the hostile ranks in one capacity or another not to interact with male members in the camps. It emphasized that such behavior would break the age-old traditions.

In reply, the girls protested the order and requested that since they had joined the hostiles, they be treated on par with male members. A few days later, a girl involved in writing the reply to Krisanisa surrendered. When I casually asked her about the correspondence, she smilingly replied, "It was just a game of boys and girls in the jungle. It ends there. I am getting married to a government servant tomorrow."

Being a non-family station and the directives by the hostile leader created its problems! There were instances of a Naga girl discarding one of her own communities and running after another, which upset the Naga men and even resorted to harassing the girl in case they were in a position of authority.

Often faced with such situations, I managed to find solutions by talking to them and guiding them to sort out their problems. It was challenging as their tribal societies were also changing!

Bamboo Dance

Chuchuyimlang (Location of Gandhi Ashram)

Gandhi Ashram Nagaland

Impur

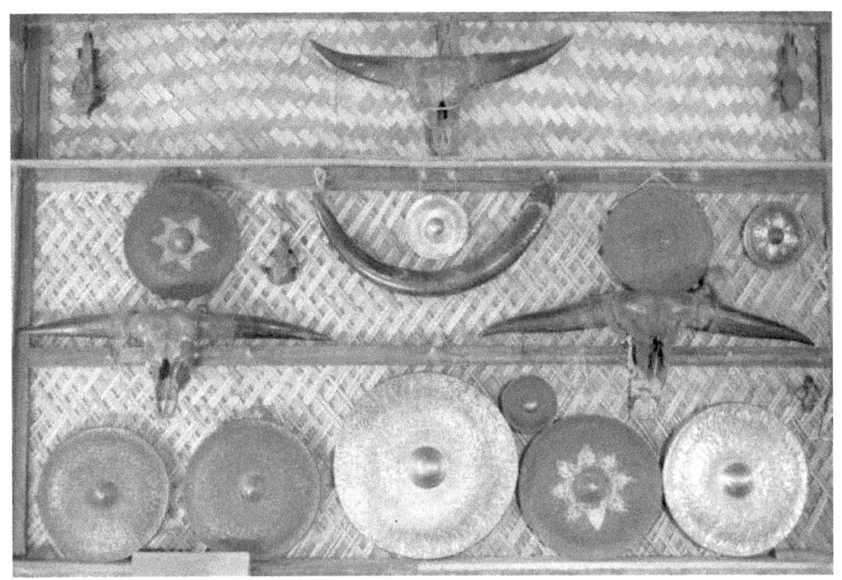

Konyak Tribe Longwa Village

Morang

Naga Morang or Communal House

Prayer Hall

Terrace Farming

21

SEMA'S ARE DIFFERENT FROM THE OTHERS

During my tour in the Sema area, we were invited to celebrations in one of the units of the security forces. Naga officials and leaders from the area also participated. Drinks flowed freely, and everyone was liberally bending their elbows. It was a hilarious party with dancing and joking all in a soldierly style.

The Subhedar Major of the unit was bent on making me drunk. To avoid it, I gently opened the subject of the influence of the General Officer Commanding at the Army Headquarters as the Chief of the Staff was his brother-in-law and emphasized that he must do everything to please and influence the General so that his unit got a good name. He agreed and asked me how to do it. I pointed to the Public Relations Officer who had accompanied me and told the major that the officer was not only in the good books of the General but also had a very great influence on him and that in fact, he had been sent to report on the unit.

Subhedar Major jumped up and had a quick powwow with other junior commissioned officers and established himself next to the Public Relations Officer, who could not understand why suddenly such attention and importance were being attached to him. Pleased with the honored position, he liberally donated 2 hundred rupees for a party with the boys attending him and was carried to his room accompanied by the song 'For He's a Jolly Good Fellow.'"

This allowed me to move freely among the gathering and talk to my Naga friends. When I sat near the Head Dobhasi (head interpreter) who had already had more than his share of rum, he complained of the sorrow and worry he was going through because he could not marry the girl he was after. I was amazed at his story, for I knew that he had grown-up children studying in schools and colleges and had sons-in-law. I gently said, "I thought you were already married! Maybe I am wrong." "No, you are correct," he replied, "I have 5 wives, sixteen children, and 6 grandchildren. But I want to marry this girl. I am prepared to pay 10 thousand rupees to her. She knows English, and I want an English-speaking secretary. I have taken several contracts but find it difficult to correspond in English."

He had sons who knew English, and he could have easily had one of them join the business. Instead of paying 10 thousand rupees for a girl, he could just as easily have hired an English-speaking secretary. When I suggested this alternative to overcome his difficulty and sorrow, he said, "True, but to have an English-speaking wife is something different. Not only will I have a young wife, but she could also accompany me during my official visits and thus add to my influence and prestige. I am an influential and wealthy man. How can she dare to refuse my hand? Though over 40, I am still young. But she says that she is in love with some college boy and will not marry an old hog like me. This insult is intolerable! I must have her!"

Having tried in vain to persuade him to discard this idea, I left him to brood over his problem. I went to another Naga friend sitting a few chairs away. He had been attentively listening to our conversation and thanked me for my advice to the Head Dobashi. "How are you concerned?" I asked him.

He replied, "The girl concerned is my daughter. I need money, and I would most welcome 10 thousand rupees. But I must care for the wishes of my daughter. She is educated and is helping me in my business. She will not marry him even if he gives 10 times as much. She is in love with a young boy and does not care for wealth. The earlier we discard the system of purchasing wives, the better."

Among Nagas, the Sema tribe was the only one where a man did not have to pay to get a wife but could possess as many wives as he wanted. The wealthier the man, the more wives he had. As a result, many of the educated Semas who had sufficient money did not have to pay for a suitable girl from other tribes in Naga Hills and Assam.

During my tour in the same area, I came across an incident where a young boy was deprived of most of his possessions in order to get a wife. While working in the fields, due to illegal intimacy, a girl became pregnant. When threatened by her parents, she named the boy. The youth had no alternative but to marry her. He had to part with three-fourths of the cows and pigs he owned and half of the land, plows, and other trenching implements. Divorce cases among the Semas were negligible as compared to other races of Nagas, where marriage and divorce were easier.

The night of the party, the Villagers and a strong detachment rushed out to help the Police. The head Dobhashi, on returning home from the party, learned from his watchers that the girl he wanted to marry had been seen closeted with her lover. Enraged, he took out his revolver and broke down the door of the girl's room, determined to shoot the boy. However, he could not find him. The girl snatched the pistol from the hands of the intoxicated head Dobhashi and, having raised an alarm, turned him out of the house at the point of the gun, which she refused to return.

At the point of the same pistol, and in the presence of his wives, children, and other locals who had gathered, she made him sign a pledge that he would neither trouble her again nor ask for her hand in marriage. Then, she handed him over to the police.

I had left the Naga Hills and was staying in Shillong, awaiting posting orders. Memories of my friends in the Naga Hills constantly came back to me, and I often thought of them and wished to know about their welfare.

One day, a noted spinster from Naga Hills came to call on us. We discussed various subjects for over 2 hours. As it was nearing lunchtime, she wished us goodbye and crossed over to the door. But there she stopped, meditated, and returned. Coming near me, she opened her purse and took out a small stone. Presenting it to me, she said, "I have brought this for you. It is from Pagala Pahar (Hill) where the signboard reads, 'Beware of rolling stones, do not stop.'" She paused for a moment, watching me.

After I thanked her for her gift, my wife curiously asked what the significance was. After repeated queries, I replied, "She considers me stone-hearted with no soft corner for her." Then turning to the visitor, I said, "If I was not married, the end of the story would have been different. But you see, I have a wife. You'll have to try somewhere else."

She departed, and I was told by residents of Naga Hills that she prays for me every day.

In some tribes, the customary way of settling a dispute among youths who are in love with the same girl is indeed novel. Both stand in front of the girl and scratch each other's faces with their fingernails. The one who bleeds and gives up the fight loses, and the one who endures wins. Youths with scratches covering their faces are a common sight. The victor or the vanquished can be assessed by whether he is accompanied or not.

Those who joined the hostile ranks and remained in the jungle were probably more influenced by Gupid Regma Lance Naik from the Indian Army, who joined the hostiles in the rank of Brigadier and set himself up as a Mongol Emperor with many girls attending him. He was subsequently tried by the hostile court when the locals lodged a complaint against him for being intimate with 6 girls. Dismissed and disillusioned, he returned to his house to be thrown out by his wedded wife.

The Naga hostiles encouraged some of the girls to entice personnel of the security forces, but their efforts were successful only on a few occasions. Other girls who were sent for this purpose took the opportunity of matrimony and left the Naga Hills to lead a peaceful life.

There was a race among educated and advanced Naga girls to marry officers of the security forces and administration. In pursuing her ambition to get an officer as a husband, a pretty girl went as far as agreeing to serve at a party partly unclothed.

There was an interesting incident during this period. A very pretty Naga girl from a rich family was in love with a non-Naga officer. It was probably her sixth love episode. The officer was proceeding to Shillong in another Naga gentleman's car when the party met with a serious accident. All the occupants were killed except the officer who was seriously injured. The doctor feared that he might expire despite the medical help rendered and requested the officer to record his last wish. The officer replied, "I wish to have a last kiss of so and so before I die."

The doctor sent an express telegram to the Deputy Commissioner stating the last wish of the injured officer and requested the Deputy Commissioner to send the officer's beloved by air, if possible. The Deputy Commissioner, much perplexed, could take no action.

22

NAGAS' SENSE OF COMMUNITY AND ABOUT THEIR WEDDINGS

To a Naga, the land is valued above everything else, a result of which all festivals in Naga land, irrespective of the tribe, relate to different seasons and the land. The main functions coincide with the beginning of the plowing season, sowing time, harvesting, and then the period of rest during the year after hard work. These festivals are celebrated very solemnly as none can afford to lose a good crop or harvest. The whole village joins in the celebration.

One of the most important points that struck me was that during one of the festivals, every family breaks its old oven and builds a new one. On that day, the food is cooked outside the house. Also on that day, a man is neither allowed to eat food cooked by the opposite sex nor drink water fetched or touched by womenfolk, and for the day, he must sleep alone outside the house.

The time and date of the functions are decided by the Head Priest who declares a "Genna" on the occasion. It is binding on both non-Christians and Christians and is strictly adhered to. Once Genna is proclaimed on a certain day, no one can cross the limits of the village.

In Naga Hills, school holidays also coincide with plowing, sowing, and harvesting seasons so that not only children can assist their parents in the fields, but teachers can also get time to work on their land.

The problem of finding laborers to plow, sow, or harvest the paddy does not exist. Everyone works on their land, which is very rarely away from the house. Further, during each season, on directions from the Head Priest, men, women, boys, and girls work in numbers on the fields of others in rotation. As a result, tilling of the land, sowing, and harvesting are completed in a quick time. All that the owner of the land is required to do is to feed the helpers at lunchtime with rice, beef or vegetables, and Madhu (rice beer).

It is a very pleasant sight to see people working in the fields, with men, women, boys, and girls forming separate teams and working facing each other, singing. One team sings a line, and then it is replied to or repeated by the opposite team. Thus, the work becomes a joy, and it indeed marks the beginning of many a romance and matchmaking effort.

While proceeding to the village of Mao on the border of the Naga Hills, I had stopped more than once to witness the charm of the cultivation and the songs sung by workers. It was indeed enchanting. But for the urgency of the work I had at Mao, I would have stayed there to watch it till dusk. In the evening, I was returning to Kohima when I saw one of my young friends walking briskly on the road with flowers in one hand and a parcel in the other. He was a fiery youth, thin and short, with a hearty laugh. I stopped him out of curiosity. He appeared to be in a great hurry. Jokingly, I asked him, pointing at the new suit he was wearing and the items in his hands, "Are you proceeding to a wedding?"

"How did you know?" he said in surprise. "You appear to know everything, but how can it be? We decided to get married only 2 hours earlier!"

"Anyway, tell me who the girl is and how it has materialized?" I asked.

He laughed, then looking at his watch, he said, "Still time! I will tell you how she agreed to marry me. We have been working together in the fields for the last week. I tell you she is a killer. As I could not do hard work, I decided to take the easier job of distributing food and Madhu. I gave her the best part of it and told her all the stories of my visit to Delhi and meeting with the Prime Minister."

After having lunch, she went to clean the utensils near a nearby spring, and I volunteered to help her. We had a lot of Madhu, danced, and sang. "You know," he continued, lowering his voice, "I kissed her too. She said we must get married immediately, and so I am on my way to the wedding altar."

I wished him good luck and left. The next day, I saw him walking alone in the bazaar. I stopped him and asked why he was alone and where his wife was. With his usual happy-go-lucky mood, he said, "Oh, it lasted only one night. We divorced at dawn. She said that under the influence of Madhu, she liked me due to my stories of Delhi and other places. But once married, she discovered that although I am intelligent, my stories are worth hearing for one night only. Physically, she did not approve of me as a husband to live with throughout life. So, we parted. There she is." He pointed to a robust and charming girl walking with another young boy. "Good luck!" he shouted to her. She just waved to him.

I left the place, saying, "So it is all that easy!"

I was invited to a wedding. I took more interest in it than usual as both parties were known to me. When I entered the church, I stopped to see the pastor who was performing the ceremony. The individual, well known to me, was adorned as a reverend and claimed himself to be one. However, not only did I have no respect for him, but I also disliked him for his domed garb of priesthood when his actions, deeds, and words were contradictory to all the preachings. I could not reconcile my mind to the fact that a man of no principles, and one who could tell lies time and again, could evoke the Almighty to bless a couple at such an important function.

Anyway, I could not turn back out of respect for the boy and the girl who were to wed. The marriage was solemnized, and we accompanied the couple to their house for further celebrations, which were being held according to the Naga customs and traditions with songs and other jubilations.

It struck me that the Naga wedding customs were akin to those in Maharashtra, despite the great distance between the 2. How could there be so much similarity? The conclusion I came to was that in the days gone by, despite the lack of communication and the great distances, there was much in common among the people of India. However, even with the advent of all types of communications, all that was common was being ignored and forgotten with the emphasis on political and economic life, and the differences were being encouraged to safeguard the interests of a certain community or the other.

The system of marriage and its celebrations in Naga Hills were not complicated. A man and a woman could take one another as husband and wife by offering a bowl of Madhu to each other or cutting a chicken for a feast in the presence of kith and kin. Divorce was equally easy, and the announcement of it was recognized by all.

The procedure for selecting a bride and bridegroom was common among all tribes except the Konyaks, and in most cases, the boys and girls made their selection and decided to marry. Among the Konyaks, the boy as well as the girl had a say, but the latter to a lesser degree. On attaining maturity, the girl was asked by her father to select a boy to be her husband. When the girl selected a boy and if he was willing, they were allowed to stay together as husband and wife without being wed for a certain period. If the girl became pregnant during the period, then the boy was accepted as a suitable husband, and the wedding took place. Failing that, they were separated, and the procedure was repeated with someone else.

Any intimacy with a married woman was viewed as an act of misconduct. But a divorced woman was free to lead a life of sexual freedom and even bear a child, provided she could name the father of the child. Children born under such circumstances were accepted as legal. The custom among Zeliang Nagas of disposing of a child whose father could not be named by the divorced woman was indeed cruel. The result was obvious.

Unmarried girls, if found to have been intimate with boys, were driven out of the village. The numerous prostitutes at Dimapur and the bordering Naga Hills were none other than such misguided girls driven out of their homes, as well as divorced women who could not find other means of livelihood.

23

POOR COMMUNICATION AND PROPHETIC VIEWS ON POST-INDEPENDENCE

Nagas were shrewd observers and seldom failed to express their views outspokenly, and even criticize without hesitation if found necessary. They were often suspicious of non-Nagas and often asked the same question repeatedly to satisfy themselves that the same answer was given.

As a measure of welfare, radio receivers were issued to the different centers in Naga Hills. All-India Radio, Guwahati, broadcasts various entertaining items in different Naga dialects.

A few months later, one of the newly appointed young officers, during his visit, asked Visar Angami and other elders whether they liked the broadcasts. Visar promptly replied, "Never heard of it." The young officer, enraged at the curt reply, belligerently shouted, "You are a drunkard. What about the others?" Visar asked all his companions and then replied, "They too haven't heard it."

"So, it appears that you are trying to boycott it. You are hostile and you are instigating others!" the officer shouted at him. Visar, who was sober, started laughing. "Don't get angry and please do not accuse us unnecessarily." With his normal ease, he added, "We want to hear it. Like anyone else, we also are fond of entertainment, but the difficulty is that we cannot hear it when we have the time and when we need entertainment."

"What do you mean? Are you trying to sugar-coat your arrogance?" shouted the officer, who was still seeing red.

"Please do not misunderstand us. Your broadcasts in the Naga dialect are from 1 P.M. to 3 P.M. when most of us are working in the fields. I have tried to tune in when I am at home. Your radio broadcasts cater to late risers, those who go to the office at 10 A.M., housewives who can stay and work in the house, and the jobless. Not only we the Nagas, but I think many people in India, get up at 4 A.M. and go to work by 6 A.M. However, broadcasts come on the air at 7 A.M. We come home from the fields and other work by 4 P.M., but the transmitters are then off the air. By the time the broadcasts resume, we are about to sleep."

"I am told by many people," Visar continued, "that not only the Prime Minister but many other leaders often speak to the nation after 8 p.m. and that important news reviews and other educative speeches are broadcast after 7 p.m., but by then, nineteen-twentieths of the nation is fast asleep. It would be better if someone entertains us, educates us, and tells us something interesting when we are awake or can afford to be near the radio set and not when we are asleep or out at work. Instead of accusing us of not listening to what you want to tell us, try to understand our habits and the psychology of common people like us. Don't expect us to listen to you at your convenience instead of forcing us." Unenlightened, the officer left the place, shouting at Visar, "I had heard that you are an idiot but never thought that you were insane!"

Visar laughed heartily and, singing a Naga song, entered a Madhu shop. Disgusted with the lack of enthusiasm shown by the people toward radio broadcasts, one of the advocates suggested a novel method of equipping the aircraft with loudspeakers to broadcast news and speeches while flying low over the villages. The experiment was carried out with great jubilation from day-to-day.

One of the aged villagers who had participated in World War II came to my office to inquire how the aircraft had started talking instead of firing, strafing, and bombing. When I explained to him what was happening and the intention behind it, he murmured, "It is too bad, big talkers do little harm. So now we need not be afraid of the aircraft."

The individual who had initiated the idea was eager to know the reaction of the people and the effect of the experiment. When he asked some educated people from the villages, one of them replied, "It was like talking through a hat. The children were so overjoyed to see an aircraft flying so low daily and without doing any harm that between the shouts of the children and the roaring sound of the engine, we heard nothing. Someone was heard shouting, but we were unable to distinguish anything clearly."

"Yes, yes," another uneducated villager hastily added, "We thought that as the plane had no horn, he was asking us to make way for it by shouting."

"You are an idiot!" the young officer exasperatedly replied. "The aircraft does not need to blow a horn to seek its way. The man in the aircraft was telling you what was good for you. It is a new way of establishing contact with the people."

"True," the first critic said. "It appears that contact through the air is gaining predominance over personal contact. Probably it is the trend of present-day politicians, who lead their parties to their graves. The hostiles survive because they have day-to-day personal contact. I am told by one of the learned men that the communists lay very great stress on personal contact and word-of-mouth communication so that what is said is heard and understood through the medium of one another. On the other hand, democratic politicians believe in the liberal idea of talking through the air to hide their poor personality so that the listener does not know the personality of the man speaking. Thus, the speaker gets the satisfaction that the whole world has listened to him without the fear of being hooted, booed, or ridiculed."

"Enough with your theory!" The officer snubbed him. "When television is introduced, you will be able to see the speaker also. True, but neither can he see the listener, nor has he an opportunity to know the reaction of the people or even know if anyone listened to him." Not content with the result, the young officer left for the next village to find out the reaction, and he returned with a report that the experiment was a success!

The Naga National Council, headed by A.Z. Phizo, had boycotted the elections to the state assembly from the 3 constituencies in Naga Hills. The majority believed in the move and supported it wholeheartedly. However, those who were willing to contest the elections were afraid of the repercussions. Phizo knew no other way to deal with the opposition than to silence them with death. During the 1957 elections, the opposition to the hostile leadership had mounted, and people felt safer due to the presence of security forces. One of them even became a Deputy Minister in the Assam Cabinet. During informal discussions, one of the educated elders complained that the disease of professionals, namely I.D.P.D., had now spread to Naga Hills as well. When I asked him what he meant by I.D.P.D., he said, "Indian Democrats Professional Disease. It has become an All-India Disease and will have to be dealt with on a war footing. It affects the power-hungry, employed and unemployed, rich and poor, men and women. It is creating conflicts and causing disintegration of parties, states, and India as a whole. I have spent many days in Assam and have seen the ultimate struggle for power going on; for getting tickets for elections, resulting in frustrations, causing defection in the parties, and so on."

He paused to light his cigarette, "It is a new profession. But unlike other services, it has no examination or selection by a board, and finally, there are no rules of conduct as applicable to other All-India Services.

The maximum punishment for any misbehavior is expulsion from the party." "Yet, a man is free to join any other party or seek re-election as an independent candidate. Tenure of duty and service, age of retirement, increment, and pension are not laid down for IDPD ambitious persons. One is not sure whether he will be appointed as a Minister. Consequently, he has 5 years of power to establish himself and not only make good fortune and earn his pension but also get suitable appointments for his kin and kin to support him when unemployed. All his actions are motivated to please his relations, supporters, and other well-wishers so that he can be re-elected once again if he gets a ticket." He stopped to light another cigarette and continued, "Once, I was present at a district headquarters when the budget for the allocation of money for road improvements was being considered. As no amount was earmarked for the muddy road leading to the police lines, the Superintendent of Police protested and requested reconsideration. The IDPD in power from the district shouted, 'You are not public. The money is meant for public roads so that the public vote for me and my party again. Yours is a government department. Ask the Government to allot funds for the repairing of roads near police lines. Only Government vehicles go on that road and not public vehicles. I am the people's representative, so I cannot release the amount being spent on roads used by Government officials only. You have no alternative but to vote for the party in power; otherwise, adverse remarks against you will be entered in your confidential report.' The humiliated Superintendent of Police left the place disgusted." He laughed heartily. Others also joined him. When silence was restored, he continued, "The hereditary customs and traditions in almost all the hill areas are somewhat different from other developed parts of India. Today, we are represented by a Gaon Bura, who is the selected elder. Everyone obeys him. To solve difficulties, he contacts the authorities and returns with a decision. He does not claim any daily allowance, traveling allowance, or monthly remuneration as is the case with I.D.P.D., M.L.A.S. The Gaon Bura depends on his cultivation and the 25 NP he annually gets per house in the village for his living."

"To begin with, if the government had formed a popular body of these Gaon Buras to meet once or twice a year to form rules and regulations, we could have gradually molded ourselves to the new democratic method of popular government. These Gaon Buras are neither educated in the modern art of winning elections nor in taking the floor to deliver speeches, but they are wise and experienced and know well what is good and bad for society." "True," another elder shouted. "Hence, those who know the modern art of grabbing power, lecturing, and arguing will get elected to either represent us or govern us. In which case, our society will get a jolt resulting in disorder. There is no doubt that educated and experienced persons must someday take the upper hand, but the process must be a gradual one. Otherwise, we will suffer the same fate as Lushai Hills where the sudden abolition of the age-old system of chieftainship, to which people owed allegiance, brought only confusion."

"There is much truth in what you said, and everyone should consider this," the first critic took a chance to add. "One of the elected members has not returned to Naga Hills since his election. I met him in Shillong the other day. He said that he was so very busy with the meetings of the select committee and the session of the house that he had no time to leave Shillong. The chief minister had taken a great liking to him due to his perspective, foresight, flexibility, generosity, clarity, and loyalty. He said that he made several broadcasts to us from All-India, but unfortunately, I never heard one. He also told me that he took full advantage of his popularity and dynamic personality to get relief in cash and kind and agriculture loans for us. This man informed me in confidence that he was insisting on getting more money for agriculture loans as it is never returned. Whenever the question of refund is raised, the agriculturists raise a hue and cry, and out of sheer fear of losing popularity and votes, time and again recovery is postponed, and ultimately these loans are written off and new ones are granted." "He has asked me to inform all his and my relatives to apply for this loan as an allotment of relief to our status."

"But it is detrimental to us," another elder shouted angrily. "It will accustom us to begging and make us lazy. There are no beggars in Naga Hills. This relief in cash and kind and loans will lead us into bad habits of dependency, and we will ask for more and more. What we want is work, payment for it, and food grains at reasonable prices in all places. The more we clamor for relief and loans, the more elected leaders will pressure the government for them with the threat that the party in power will lose popularity. The government will have no alternative but to grant such loans on one hand and increase taxes on the other. As more political parties are formed in Naga Hills, this game of maintaining cheap popularity will increase, making people shy away from labor and hard work. Many of the young circle officers are already following the policy of IDPD members to increase their influence over locals at the cost of society's progress and the nation's wealth by pressing the government to give more relief in cash and kind to the villagers in their jurisdiction."

"Indeed, indeed," the first critic shouted. "I wonder if anyone has collated the total amount spent by the Governors, Ministers, MLAs, and honorary workers of other social organizations on remuneration, daily allowance, traveling allowance, cars, free accommodation, receptions, and loans that are never to be recovered. Probably it will be more than half the budget of India and more than the defense budget. And yet the conflict, under one form or another, instigated by members of the IDPD corps to gain power for an individual and party is tearing society into pieces." The discussion would have probably continued, but I had to attend a trunk call from Shillong, so I left the discussions. The formation of a separate state of Naga

Hills-Tuensang Area had led many leaders to dream of occupying Ministerial chairs for which there was no provision yet. As a result, propaganda demanding that the Naga leaders must have a full share in the administration was undertaken. Many citizens sincerely believed in this line of thought and felt that, without it, they could not achieve prosperity. It was amusing to see the prospective ministers building support for themselves.

24

THE NEW REALITY, THE COST OF DEMOCRACY EXPLAINED

One day, the group of elders who had previously come to the office for discussions turned up again, with a few additional members, and requested me to spare enough time to clarify some of their doubts. Once they settled down comfortably, they started asking one another to speak. It was very common that when a group of people came either to represent something or for discussion, the chosen person, out of respect and regard for others, would ask others to speak first. Only when the other members requested him once again would he begin to speak.

Once this routine formality was over, their spokesman put forward his points: "When the new state of Naga Hills-Tuensang Area was carved out of Assam and the Northeast Frontier Agency, the Government undertook the responsibility of providing funds to bear all the expenditure of the administration and development. Will this arrangement continue indefinitely? If a popular Government with Ministers, Deputy Ministers, parliamentary secretaries, and a full-fledged secretariat with a big staff comes into existence, who will bear the additional expenditure on this account? Will the Central Government provide all the funds to balance the increasing debt, or will it have to be raised by the state by levying taxes that do not exist?"

It was a difficult question to answer. So far, the inhabitants of Naga Hills paid no taxes except the solitary house tax of one rupee per house per year, and everyone feared that any change in the administration would bring forth additional taxes. I told them that the question could best be answered either by the authorities in Delhi or the prospective ministers among themselves. However, at the same time, I cautioned them that the possibility of the government bearing all the expenditure forever was remote, and a state with a popular government would have to find ways and means to raise funds from the local resources to meet at least part of the additional recurring expenditure of the ever-expanding administrative machinery. Administrative machinery, once assembled, continues to expand with an increasing demand every year of extra staff."

My words gave rise to cross-currents and forgetting the purpose for which they had come to my office, they started discussing among themselves. One of the gray-haired elders shouted, "I cannot understand why we require so many people to administer us. Even before and after the independence of India, we had only one Deputy Commissioner and a few Naga officers as assistants to the Deputy Commissioner. We had our village and Tribal Councils. We decided what was best for us and approached the Deputy Commissioner directly to get his sanction. But now we have a Deputy Commissioner for each district with so many additional Deputy Commissioners, Circle officers, and whatnot, and a commissioner above them. I am told that the commissioner must take approval from the Governor. Now you say we will have Ministers and a secretariat. Unless we are educated as to whom we should approach, we will become lost in our own land."

"My problem is a bigger one," an elderly Gaon Bura said loudly. "So far, we have been worrying about receiving the Commissioner and the Deputy Commissioner. Now, there will be so many Ministers, Secretaries, and heads of departments. Our Naga Hill is so small, and all of them must tour to show that they are working. How will I know who? Plus, to receive them all will take half of my time every day."

One of the educated and elderly leaders said, "We cannot condemn all that is being done, but I get puzzled to see the way it is done. I have been to Delhi before Independence and recently also. Then for the whole undivided India, there was only one secretariat building. Now there are 10 or more, yet they say that offices are overcrowded and require additional accommodation. The same is the case in Shillong. In addition to the old secretariat buildings, a new palatial one has been built, and hundreds of residential houses are being hired to accommodate offices. If that happens in Kohima, we, the villagers, will have no place in and around Kohima."

One of the advocates of self-rule who cherished the hope that he would someday become a Minister tried to explain to them the importance of having additional "Ministers and self-government." Everyone agreed with him on the importance of self-rule and the democratic method of governing people but could not agree on the expanding nature of the administrative machinery.

Visar Angami, who so far was sitting silently as a spectator, shouted, "We must have a democratic popular government, but I only hope that our Ministers will do something practical instead of delivering lectures, presiding over various functions, and spending time on informal discussions and free advice in the house and at public places at any time. I have collected records of a friend of mine who is a Minister. He delivered in a year 92 speeches, presided over functions including the social gatherings of lower/primary schools on 60 occasions, and gave a press interview every time he left headquarters. I cannot understand how a man who becomes a Minister suddenly gets invested with divine and technical powers to speak day and night on any subject. Now, no longer a Minister, he has lost all his divine powers."

"No more does he deliver speeches; no more does he preside over functions; no longer do the schoolboys turn out and garland him.

Earlier, the Deputy Commissioner used to be in attendance whenever my friend, as a minister, visited the district headquarters. Now my friend must wait for hours before he can meet the Deputy Commissioner!"

At this stage, one of the elders abruptly interrupted with a question, "I am told that there are schools where Civil and Military officers undergo training before they join service. Are there any schools to train the Ministers also?" I burst out laughing at his innocence and ignorance.

Visar Angami took the floor again. "No, there are none. The secretaries, who hail from the Indian Administrative Service and those experienced, educate the newcomers secretly. Anyway, I was wondering why an enterprising publisher has not taken the trouble to publish volumes of speeches delivered by all the Ministers since 1947. It would be an interesting series of contradictions, humor, and new ideas for the future politicians as 'dos and don'ts.'"

One of the youngsters shouted at Visar, "It appears that you know everything about Ministers, Ministries, and the formation of the popular Government. Tell me, what special qualifications do Ministers in all the states have that I don't possess? Can I become a Minister?"

An unperturbed Visar replied, "You can become one, and you have all the qualifications of a minister but one. You do not have a hold over the masses in your area to threaten the would-be chief minister and upset the equilibrium in the parliamentary groups of the party that may be chosen by the people to form the government. This reminds me of a story told to me by one officer. At a dinner, one of the ministers came very late and unaccompanied by his wife. When the hostess inquired, the minister replied, "What to do! There is not a single domestic servant in the house."

"All have left for one reason or another," Visar said. Then, turning to the Inspector General of Police, who happened to be the host, the minister asked him to help him find some domestic servants. The Inspector General flickered with mischief and replied, "Sir, just wait. I will phone all my Deputy Inspector Generals of Police and the Superintendents of Police in the state. I will let you know the result in a few minutes!" The Inspector General returned after a few minutes to report that the problem of domestic servants was acute all over the state and that even his officers had to do all the work, including sweeping houses. "But sir," the Inspector General continued, "my officers said that if there was a vacancy for a minister in the state or center, they could bring 10 volunteers every minute to work even on half the existing pay."

There was laughter. The youngster replied, "It was imprudent of the Inspector General to reply as he did. If I had been the Minister, I would have sacked him the next moment!" One elder replied, "Try it when you become a Minister." Then turning to Visar, he asked, "When the people elect their representatives to form a popular government, why is it that every moment some agitation or movement is going on against this popular government?"

Visar laughed and replied, "There are 2 reasons. One is that when the cabinet is sworn in and everyone is sure of their seat, they either become dictators who ignore the common good or, in trying to please others, they may try to be saints and cause a vacuum that turns out to be a weakness. The second is that some of the disgruntled ones try to unseat those in power so that they can become ministers by agitating the minds of others and developing it into a movement."

It appeared that they had lost track of the purpose for which they came to my office. To put an end to it, I told them to study the system of popular government carefully and then drew their attention to the enormous amounts of food grains collected by the hostile Nagas from them as subscriptions, donations, and fines, either with their consent or at the point of a bayonet!

I summed it up this way! "Now that you are accustomed to parting with money, you should not be worried about taxes being levied by the popular government! Anyway, these would not exceed the amount collected by the hostile Nagas."

25

HOSTILES USED CHURCHES FOR THEIR ACTIVITIES

Miss Belieu Chase, niece of Angami Zao, and a noted person for her interest in the church, was impressed by Reverend Benjamin, who I learned was the pivot of the Revivalist movement and had achieved fame, it was said, for curing people in the name of Christ. With due permission of the authorities, she brought him to tour Naga Hills, and he was experimenting at different places with his divine powers. His presence had already stirred the church leaders in Naga Hills, and many were trying to get him removed. Miss Belieu came to the office to invite me to meet the Reverend. I politely declined to go. So, she brought him, his adopted daughter, and his son to meet me. I had indeed a very interesting conversation with him, as during my school days, I had studied scripture and had attained a very high proficiency. Thereafter, I had many meetings with him in my office.

He had just returned from his tour of the Lotha area and was to leave for Imphal in the next few days. Suddenly, he turned up in my office one evening and requested me to arrange an appointment with an army dentist and physician, as he had a toothache, and his daughter was suffering from acute constipation. I did arrange for their treatment. His tooth was extracted. But I could not reconcile my mind to this role of curing persons with just faith and the desire to cure himself and his adopted daughter by a Doctor of Medicine. Time and again, I asked myself why he did not cure himself and his daughter with his divine powers.

When I tried to express my feelings to my friend, he said, "Please stop! Never ask questions or express doubts about the powers, contradictory expressions, and behavior of big people. Having attained a certain position of standing, they inherit a birthright to contradict themselves. To express doubts is a means to ruin oneself." I am not a Christian by faith and religion, but the church has always fascinated me as I was educated in a school conducted by Christian missionaries. I had studied the Bible in detail and often, in the company of school friends, attended sermons in the church. What I liked best was the solemnity, cleanliness, and the fact that all those who attended the service showed no distinction of rank and file, poor and rich, and attained the natural way of being equal in the presence of God. Despite all my liking for the church, by faith, I remained a Hindu, for in the message of the Almighty as preached in the Gita and the Bible, I saw no difference.

The church and the pastors played an important part among those Nagas who had become Christians. Unlike other parts of India, one thing was very noticeable. Those Nagas who became Christians by faith considered themselves superior to those who had not embraced Christianity. In many villages, Nagas who had embraced Christianity lived separately and established Christian Khels (suburbs).

Also, a few of the foreign missionaries and some local Naga ministers indulged in politics and incited the locals against the government. Personalities like Reverend Kizungliba Ao were above everything. The hostile leaders made religion a matter of propaganda to incite those Nagas who were Christians by faith. Mr. Inkongmeren Ao, Vice President of the defunct Naga National Council, time and again propagated that he was trying to form a "Far Eastern Christian State," irrespective of the fact that even today 50 percent of the Nagas are not Christians by faith. Angami Zapu Phizo went as far as proclaiming that Christianity was in danger and that everyone should rise to protect it from Hindus in India.

To begin with, locals believed in his propaganda, but soon it became evident that it was the hostiles who were polluting the sacred church by their acts. They fired from the churches on the security forces, held conferences in the churches, used the altar to hide arms, and looted property. The instances where the hostiles obstructed and looted persons proceeding to Bible conferences and religious congregations arranged by the church of Naga Hills were innumerable and were condemned by Revs. Kizungliba Ao and Longri Ao.

On the contrary, officers of the Security Forces who were Christians never missed an opportunity to conduct services in churches where the local pastors had either joined the hostile ranks or deserted the villages due to fear of hostiles. The false propaganda initiated by Zapur Phizo and his stalwarts came to an end when a team of the American Baptist Mission, led by Reverends Kizungliba Ao and Longri Ao and comprising Christian ministers of the churches from each tribe, undertook an extensive tour of Naga Hills not only to restore peace but to expose the lie behind the false propaganda.

However, the efforts made by the church leaders were short-lived. The pro-hostile leaders who had a say in the church started the revivalist movement after the annual conference held by the American Baptist Mission at Jorhat in 1958, which was attended by over 600 Naga representatives. Taking advantage of the discussion on the subject in the conference, the ball of the movement was set rolling in Naga Hills by interested persons. Soon it reached a fanatic state, despite the efforts made by the church leaders to counteract it. Many Christian Naga avoided the church and started praying in the jungle.

26

THE REVIVALIST MOVEMENT AND AN OUT - SPOKEN REVEREND

I was camping in Phek and couldn't sleep until dawn due to the noise created by the revivalists in the nearby village. Out of curiosity, I went to see what was happening. Men, women, boys, and girls had gathered there, making fantastic body movements and shouting. It reminded me of the many Red Indian dances shown in films. None could hear what was being said. On the dais, a boy and a girl were shouting that the spirit had entered their soul. They were performing acrobatics.

It was a great contrast to the peaceful, pious, and soothing atmosphere in the church. I returned to my bed unable to understand this new method of praying.

The next day, as I was returning to Kohima, I saw a long line of couples, a boy and a girl, walking hand in hand with a pack of clothes on their back. Out of curiosity, I stopped near a group and asked them where they were going. They replied, "The spirit of God had entered into us. We are to carry His message up to the end of Naga Hills." I wished them, "God bless you and put you on the right path."

While I was working in my office, an educated and elderly Naga who was a Christian by faith walked in. I knew him, but he took the trouble to introduce himself again by narrating his life and all that he had done. In the end, he declared himself a good Christian.

On hearing his last sentence, I was tempted to ask him who had told him that he was a good Christian! He promptly replied, "No one. I know that I am a good Christian, and so I claim to be one." This developed into an unpleasant discussion for him. I reminded him of many chapters from the Holy Scripture and the saying that it was for others to acknowledge by conduct, piousness, character, knowledge, and humane and kind behavior of one with others that he was a real and good Christian. One who claimed it himself could be either a fraud or sent by Satan.

He was rather enraged at the onslaught. Gathering his courage, he said, "I have advanced in age. I know what I am and claim to be one of the good Christians. By profession, I am a Doctor of Medicine, and, with experience, I claim to be a good doctor. Do you agree?"

"Though I have had no occasion to consult you for treatment, I am inclined to accept you as a good doctor. But you must remember that your knowledge of being a good Doctor of Medicine has risen from 2 factors. The first one is that, after you studied medicine, you submitted yourself for examination by those who were more qualified than you and who certified that you were fit to administer medicines. Even then, you could not claim to be a proficient and good doctor, but due to your correct diagnosis and administering of medicine, people developed faith in you and started coming to you for consultation when they became ill."

It is the people who certified you and acclaimed you as a good doctor. It is the knowledge that people have faith in you, as far as medicines are concerned, which has made you consider yourself a good doctor. Despite your doctorate in medicine, could you claim to be a good physician if people had not developed faith in you and come to you for consultation and treatment?"

"What you say is true," he replied reluctantly.

"Similarly, have people told you that you are a good Christian? Have they developed faith in you due to your behavior, kindness, piety, and deeds? I am not a Christian, but neither do I claim to be one, as I feel that I am yet very, very short of all the ideals set out by God in his message to mankind in the Gita and the Scriptures." - The doctor kept silent for a minute.

It appeared that he did not like my words. Then slowly he said, "It appears you do not respect age!" I told him in a firm voice, "I do, one must. But I cannot call every elder a good Christian. It should not be interpreted as disrespect for elders."

"You are a hard nut to crack," he said, ending the discussion on the subject. "I came to request you to preach in the church this coming Sunday."

I was not surprised at the invitation. On a few previous occasions, some individuals had approached me for this purpose. With due apologies, I regretted my inability as I did not consider myself either worthy or proficient in devotion, study, and behavior to interpret the word of God and preach it to others. He differed from me and emphasized that anyone could preach the word of God and insisted on my accepting the invitation. I could not. I told him that, in my humble opinion, only those who had devoted themselves to the study of the religious books, who understood the interpretation of each word of the message therein, and who brought this into practice could claim a right to preach God's message in a church to others. Unfortunately, I could not qualify in all these, however much I wished, due to my service and being engrossed in worldly affairs.

He was rather upset on hearing my words. Getting up, he said, "I wanted you to come to the church, preach, and realize that Christ is the only Savior, and it is only he who can bring salvation to human beings. One who does not believe in him will not receive salvation, which is not far off."

I had heard it before. I accompanied him to the exit door. "I have attended prayer meetings in Mandir, Gurudwara, Masjid, and Church. I felt the presence of God everywhere. I do believe in Christ as an incarnation of God who had come to Earth to guide erring human beings, but I could not accept that only those who believe in Him could get salvation." I wished him goodbye.

Whenever I'm in Mokokchung, I never miss an opportunity to visit the house of Reverend Kigunlibs Ao at the Impur Mission Compound and hear the soothing voice and words of the Reverend.

Austerity prevailed in the house. The atmosphere was very calm, quiet, and pious, and I always felt the presence of God there. Mrs. Kizungliba, a simple but dignified lady, was a mother to everyone. Every movement of theirs was so graceful and dignified that a visitor carried memories of them forever. Neither sorrow nor joy ever brought any reflections on their graceful and very pleasant and sober faces.

Many a day, they had passed with only one meal, but they went about their work with joy and never-ending enthusiasm. In his house, not only individuals like me but also hostile Nagas and persons of small and big reputations and different religious faiths found solace.

With the habit of careful study and knowledge of the correct path of life, he had firm convictions of his own, and nothing would deviate him from them. His courage, born out of a conviction of a rightful cause and faith in the supernatural being, was admirable. On numerous occasions when he condemned the hostiles for loot, murder, and arson, and openly contradicted the hostile propaganda of schools that Christianity was in danger, and proclaimed that only the government in the land was the one now in existence, the hostiles threatened him at the point of a gun.

But he did not hesitate to repeat his firm views time and again. On many occasions, he undertook hazardous missions to meet top-ranking hostile leaders to convince them of the error they were making. Frequently, these leaders, out of sheer fright to face a domineering personality like him, avoided meeting him. It did not disappoint him, for he was convinced that someday he would be able to meet them and convince them of the right path they should follow.

Even today, though I am many miles away from the Naga Hills, the figures of Reverend and Mrs. Kizuliba often appear before me as true Ministers of Almighty God. When I need peace and mental comfort, I imagine myself sitting in their house, one like which I have yet to come across, and I feel happy and elevated out of my sorrows and difficulties.

27

RADIO CEYLON POPULAR WITH OUR YOUTH; OUR FORGOTTEN HEROES

Since I came to Naga Hills, except for the news in the morning and music late at night before going to bed, I had no opportunity to listen to the radio receiver. Often, I could not listen to the news broadcast and depended upon my staff to convey important happenings to me later in the day.

On one Sunday, I was in a holiday mood, and friends, Nagas and non-Nagas who were birds of the same feather, had flocked to my office-cum-residence. Someone suggested that the radio be switched on. The radio was tuned to the Commercial Broadcasting Station in Sri Lanka. It was nearing 10 a.m. I was not surprised that the Ceylon commercial broadcasting station should be tuned in. Probably this station, which broadcasted music in Hindi and English, was the most popular practically in every house in India, although more than 50 transmitters were broadcasting music in India.

The main reason for the popularity of the Ceylon radio transmitter was that it broadcasted light music, which could be heard anywhere in the remotest corner of India without interruption from boring speeches, and at a listener's convenience. I have often wondered why, despite India's richness in musicians and artists, people preferred to tune in to Radio Ceylon for entertainment and listen to music that was originally recorded in India. There could be more than one reason for this phenomenon.

As far as I am concerned, I like to hear classical and light music in Marathi from Maharashtra, but even with the most powerful radio receivers, the transmitter stations in many cities like Pune and Nagpur could not be picked up. Occasionally, I could catch these stations after 9 PM, but often, it was speeches that, though important, were boring at that late hour after a day's hard work. I always wondered why All-India Radio did not exclusively use a dozen powerful transmitters, each exclusively broadcasting music in one language and accessible anywhere in India.

One day, when I tuned into Ceylon radio, instead of the usual music, I heard a dreary sermon being broadcast. At first, I thought that the radio receiver was tuned to the wrong station. I called Roy to correct the error, but he confirmed that the radio was properly tuned and further enlightened me that it was a commercial broadcast on Christianity, featured for 10 minutes every day in different languages.

I wondered what it could be because it would not be an item of entertainment value. Also, the possibility of religion being advertised as a commodity by a commercial broadcasting station was remote. Further, it was inopportune to deliver a worldwide sermon at that hour. For the next few days, I tried to listen to these broadcasts regularly. To my surprise, I found that their purpose was to advertise religion, an unheard of thing.

A religion was being commercialized, and people were being allured to embrace Christianity through this medium. I could not conclude whether it was a degradation or demoralization of the preachers of a faith.

I called Roy and told him to listen to it regularly as it was likely that sponsors of the move may go to the extent of starting another "Binaca Hit parade" to popularize the religion. If listened to, the chance of salvation would disappear forever for everyone in the world!

One day, one of my staff, who had returned after a morning round of Kohima town, told me that a Naga wearing a military medal had caused a stir in the town. He had approached some of the shopkeepers to assist him financially by giving him work as he had neither a job nor could he cultivate due to disturbances, and he could not beg on the road to earn his livelihood. Members of the security forces had gathered around him and not only called him an impostor but also told him to stop wearing the medal. The individual insisted that he had been awarded the Military Cross for his outstanding bravery during World War II and as such, he could not bow down to their threats and discard it.

I brought him to my office. After questioning him, it was verified from the records kept in the office of the Deputy Commissioner that he was a member of the V forces. Single-handedly, he had penetrated the headquarters of a Japanese formation and having beheaded the commander of the force, returned with proof.

There were a few other Nagas who had also received military decorations. The late Prem Bahadur Lam, K.C., was among the recipients of the award. Born of a Gorkha father and an Angami mother, he had become a domiciled Naga still retaining the Gorkha name. In April 1956, Prem Bahadur undertook a mission to Phekhrima village, near Kohima, to assure the locals of protection from the Government. While returning, he was shot dead by the Naga Hostiles. The late Dr. Haralu was also a recipient of decorations in World Wars I and II.

While others received cash rewards attached to their awards, the individual in question did not receive any. Encouraged by his deeds during the war, he became a terror to people and took to head-hunting, with the result that his cash reward was held up. With advanced age, he had become a peaceful citizen and had taken to farming.

I questioned him concerning his future. He replied, "I want to lead a peaceful life and earn by cultivation, but due to disturbances, I cannot do it. The hostiles are pressing me to join them as a general. But I do not like the idea. My record is such that, despite this decoration, the Government will not trust and offer me a job. No alternative is left for me but to beg for alms unless someone gives me work. It will be shameful if I have to beg to display this medal."

As a member of the armed forces, I felt uncomfortable at the idea of him begging with that coveted medal pinned on his chest. I tried to find ways and means to assist him. Ultimately, I called the administrative officer of my office and gave instructions that he should be appointed a constable effective immediately.

The next day, he turned up to clarify his work. I told him that there was no specific assignment for him. He could do anything but beg. I further instructed him to go home and come on payday to collect his pay. To solve his immediate difficulty, an advance was given to him.

He stood there dumbfounded for a few minutes, then said, "To accept money without work is a difficult proposition. Anyway, I will prove my worth for the kindness shown by you." Saying so, he left.

I was surprised to see him early the next morning, standing in front of my office with 2 rifles. I asked him how he had procured them. He replied, "I am old, but I am more experienced. On the way, I met 2 hostile Nagas. I brought them with the rifles to surrender."

28

DEALING WITH HOSTILES WHO WERE KEEN TO MEET

The post-Naga People's Convention period gave considerable relief to the villagers due to the inactivity of the Naga hostiles. I visited different places to assess the attitude of the people and their requirements, if any. Upon getting the news that I was to visit Nerhema, residents of the Northern Angami area had collected there to meet me. Some of the leaders of the convention who were touring the area joined me en route.

The gathering was mainly of adults from 6 villages. As I alighted from the vehicle, Shri Mehta, a genuine social worker of Nerhema, told me that some hostile Nagas wanted to meet me and sought permission. I told him that I would be happy to meet them and assured them that they would not be arrested and could speak privately to me or openly in front of all the people without any restriction.

The news that the hostile Nagas were expected caused a little stir among the official circle, and the local commander of the Security Forces ordered protection parties to take position near the gathering. I persuaded him to withdraw all the personnel of the Security Forces from the vicinity of the meeting place. In turn, I agreed that he and his officers could attend the discussion provided they were unarmed. I also suggested to the spokesman of the elders that the presence of the hostile Nagas would be a good opportunity to discuss any doubts, and so the formal talk or discussion should be postponed until their arrival. He too welcomed the suggestion.

It was an interesting moment for me as I moved about talking to the elders and youths whom I knew. At the same time, I was trying to assess the importance of this meeting and what conversation it would lead to. At the farthest corner, I saw smoke and several men and women gathered there. As I walked to the place, I realized that food was being cooked there for a community feast for all the participants of the meeting. The atmosphere there was indeed joyful, with men joking and women singing traditional folk songs. It was indeed praiseworthy that such an event could foster goodwill.

To be convincing, conversations had to be precise and to the point, with examples; otherwise, they were always doubted. Furthermore, I had made it a point to know the characteristics of most of the people with whom I had to deal and that knowledge of their domestic circumstances, difficulties, likes, and dislikes paid dividends. During a conversation with one individual, I tried to extract some interesting points about the next man I was to meet, and it gave me a sound foundation to start a conversation with him on pleasing terms. Finally, a prompt reply to any of their questions was important. Their simplicity made knowledge of child psychology and methods of dealing with a child useful and derived successful results. The most important point in getting the respect of a child, essential to parents so that the child obeys them and grows up in a disciplined way under their guidance, is the firm conviction that his parents, especially the father, know everything and can reply to any of his questions promptly. This knowledge played the most important part in establishing and exercising one's influence in any tribal area. Love, sympathy, and firm dealing played an equally important part.

The villagers were happy that due to the convention, they were less harassed by the hostiles, and they could move freely. Also, they would not be forced to part with money and food grains to maintain the hostiles.

As we were talking informally, the pastor of the village who had gone underground with the hostile Nagas walked in. He was accompanied by a few underground political workers.

I watched the gathering. Nearly 5 hundred villagers, all adults, had gathered and were sitting in the center. The hostile Nagas were on one flank, the convention leaders in front of the villagers facing them, the officers of the Security Forces and civil administration on another flank, and 2 chairs for the elder who was the chairman, and myself, were kept in the midst of them.

I told the chairman that since the elders and leaders of the convention with all shades of opinion were present there, it would be appropriate if they carried on the proceedings on their own, and I would speak, if necessary, at the end. Saying so, I pulled my chair to a corner.

The inaugural speech of the chairman was followed by that of the convention leaders. The elder who acted as chairman emphasized the need for peace so that villagers could cultivate undisturbed. The leaders of the convention narrated the account of the meeting between the Naga delegation and the Prime Minister in Delhi, and having laid stress on the necessity of peace, assured them of a change from the past and better living conditions under the new setup.

I keenly watched the reactions of the audience. The elders and villagers did not react to their faces. The hostile Nagas were seen to consult with one another on certain points mentioned by the speakers. The officers of the administration and Security Forces were seen listening with interest. One virtue the Nagas possess is that they never interrupt a speaker. They listen patiently; however, their opinions may differ. In the end, they may either speak to express their views or ask questions to clarify certain points and assert something mentioned earlier.

The leader of the hostile Nagas declined to speak when given an opportunity on the plea that he had not been authorized to make any statement. However, he thanked everyone for allowing him and his companions to participate.

Then, as usual, the chairman asked the villagers either to speak or ask any questions. One elder, who was alleged by other elders to be pro-hostile, stood up and asked the interpreter to draw my attention as he wanted to ask me a question. As I signaled my readiness, he said, "Every one of the speakers said that since the holding of the convention, things have changed, and we may expect better conditions and life under the new setup. I am not convinced. Can you quote at least one concrete example to confirm it and convince me and other villagers?"

"It is for you to notice it and not for me to show or tell it to you," I replied promptly. "Don't you notice anything here to convince yourself?"

"No," the questioner replied.

"It is because you have a prejudiced mind," I said slowly so that the interpreter could translate each sentence properly. "If you keep your mind open to change and form the habit of seeing and noting good points rather than only the bad ones, you would have noticed the evident changes stated by the speakers. The fact that at an unarranged and not pre-organized gathering like this, the elders and the villagers, be they loyal, pro-hostile, or sitting on the fence, the convention leaders who were dubious of their security, and the hostile Nagas who dared not come out openly in the presence of the security forces for fear of arrest, could sit and eat together like brothers, free men, to express their views freely, is not only a very important indication but a concrete example of the change mentioned by the speakers."

"True!" shouted the elder. "I accept the statement of the speakers as true. You have convinced us of it," the elder said. Then, addressing the villagers and the hostile Nagas, he made a lengthy speech appealing to them to maintain peace so that everyone, including the new state, could prosper.

Afterwards, a few elders spoke in the same strain. I was requested to address the gathering, but I politely declined because various speakers had covered more points than I could wish to say. Then, I thanked everyone for coming together and promised to convey their difficulties to the administrator for appropriate action.

29

PEOPLE WHO MEAN WELL, GET SUCKED INTO COMPLEX SITUATIONS

After the feast, I looked for Mehta but could not find him. As I sat in the jeep, the Pastor and a few hostiles approached to inquire whether they could stay in the village peacefully. I told them to go through the formality of surrender and introduced them to the Commander of the Security Forces for acceptance of their surrender.

As I was about to leave the outskirts of the village on my way to Wokha, I saw Mehta standing there. I stopped to thank him for all the arrangements. He smiled and asked me when I was expected to return to Kohima. "Tomorrow," I replied. "I want to meet you there and tell you something in confidence," he said calmly. "I feel that I may not live long. Someone may try to murder me."

His words caused me a great deal of anxiety. He was rarely wrong in his deductions of events and anticipation of things to happen. I told him to take care of himself until we met the next day at Kohima and left for Wokha. All along the way, I wondered why anyone would want to murder him as he had honorably served the people and the state very sincerely and faithfully. What could it be? I must save him. These thoughts kept hovering in my mind.

"Mehta was shot dead by unknown culprits after dusk on the outskirts of the village when returning from shikar, and his gun was snatched away." This was the message I received from the officer of my department at

Norhema. It cast a gloom in my office, and so did the circle of Mehta's friends. I never expected that his end was to come so fast.

I recalled the day I had returned from Wokha in the evening. Mehta was waiting for me. Without going through the mail received in my absence, as was my procedure on return from the tour, I went to my office room with him and, having ordered tea for myself, offered him rum. I wanted to open the subject of his safety after a few minutes, but before that, he touched on the subject.

"Sir, you are aware that for the well-being of my people, I have worked most faithfully at the risk of my life, and I have never been disloyal to the Government. I worked without remuneration. It is only due to my efforts that so many hostiles from our Northern Angami area have surrendered, so many arms recovered, and the villagers have been resettled in their villages and at places of safety."

He paused to have a sip from the glass and then continued, "I am not a government servant, but I enjoyed the confidence of the district authorities more than any other government servant in the area. As a result, the responsibility of distributing relief rice and clothes has been delegated to me. People have full confidence in me. A year earlier, most of the hostiles threatened my life, but now I fear none except one. I have been to meet them in the jungle so often. I could persuade many of them to abandon their violent activities."

He had become very emotional. He paused, emptied his glass of rum, lit a cigarette, and then continued, "It appears that I will be murdered, either by my people or by that one hostile leader whom I cannot trust. They want me to keep quiet about the misdeeds that have been covered up by lies. I am the only witness to these important misdeeds, which, if revealed, may harm the reputation and service of some important persons. It seems that those who misbehave, commit crimes for their benefit, and do not value the truth must survive and prosper, while the others perish."

Mehta got up, filled his glass, and sat down again. He tried to light his cigarette, but his hands were trembling. I helped him light it and patted his hand. He was cold, and fear had seized him. I held the glass near his lips, and he took a few sips. I sat near him and said, "Don't be afraid. Tell me what has happened. Who is after you, and how have you been led into this? Trust me. We will be able to find a way out."

"It is difficult," he said, gripping my hand. "I cannot tell anyone. I am afraid to confide in you, even though I know that you are my trusted friend and will never betray me. They warned me that death would be the penalty if I spoke anything to anyone, including you. They know that you like me and have warned me that you are their real enemy, as nothing will deter you from informing the highest authorities about it if you come to know of it. But even if I do not tell anyone, I am convinced that they will murder me so that each one of them can live and prosper. So, at least someone in this world should know for what I died."

Though I was unsure of what it all related to, suddenly it struck me that it must have something to do with the reports I had received from the area. To comfort Mehta and encourage him to speak out, I said, "Perhaps I know something about it. It relates to an officer, the Naga girl working as his mistress, misappropriation of relief rations and other goods, and the receipt of those goods by the hostiles. Am I correct?"

He gazed at me with surprise in his eyes. "You know it?" he said with excitement. "Have you informed the higher authorities?" "Yes, in a guarded way," I replied. "Then I must tell you everything. At least it will relieve me of a burden, and even if I die, at least I will have the satisfaction that someone knows the truth."

He warmed up and, having lit a cigarette, continued, "The secret which I am supposed to guard has 2 parts. The first is the question of arms, and the other is rations." He went on, "You are aware that from my area, a very large number of hostile Nagas abandoned their violent activities. All of them surrendered with arms and ammunition. But the fact about the surrender of arms and ammunition has been kept hidden. As a result, the higher authorities are not happy about the surrender, and those who surrendered are being repeatedly questioned about the disposal of arms and ammunition and where such material is kept hidden. They are pressuring me to tell the truth that they surrendered with arms and ammunition. I have kept a record of it. At the same time, the officer threatened me not to inform the authorities that these hostiles had surrendered their weapons. "Where are the arms and ammunition? How has the material been disposed of?" I queried anxiously.

"The arms and ammunition are safe and in the custody of the district authorities at Kohima, but they have been forwarded differently," he replied. "Most often when a patrol went out, it was stated in the morning situation report, irrespective of whether they encountered Naga hostiles or not, that there was a heavy encounter. Fictitious figures of hostiles killed and wounded were recorded, but their bodies could not be recovered as these were believed to have been carried away by other hostile Nagas. In addition, figures for the number of arms and ammunition recovered were quoted. Then arms and ammunition equal to that quoted in the report were forwarded from the accumulated stock of surrendered arms and ammunition."

"What is this game? Is it to get credit?" I asked him. "Yes. The officer told me that a report about the surrender of arms by hostiles brings credit to none except those Nagas who were hostile. On the contrary, by the procedure adopted by him, not only would he bring credit to his unit, but it is likely that some of the men under his command would get the Ashoka Chakra or some such award for gallantry and devotion to duty. Each weapon captured earned a point toward winning the trophy to be awarded by the General Officer Commanding to the unit which recovered the largest number of arms and ammunition during the year."

"Unbelievable, but I accept it as true since you have told me," I said, for I knew by experience that he would not tell a lie. "It is true, very true. There is something more to it. Every time the patrol returned, the officer made me sign a report stating that his summary report of hostiles killed and wounded was confirmed as correct by my informants. To begin with, I protested the procedure, but he told me that it was a common practice followed by all other units, and if he did not follow suit, his unit would lose its good name. He also told me that the units in the Sema and Zeliang areas had arrested a few Nagas who were armorers and experts in the manufacture of single or double-barrelled muzzle-loading guns."

The units were bringing pipes from the plains area and getting muzzle-loading guns manufactured so that these could be sent to higher authorities as captured during action now and then. He told me to get an armorer of that caliber and also get pipes. I failed, and he is angry with me."

I shuddered upon hearing it. I would have discarded it as a lie, but some of the reports I had received earlier had indicated that some such things were being cooked up. One day, when I was sitting in my office discussing the situation with Shri S.M. Dutt, I.P., one of the commanding officers, came to request help. He wanted 2 rifles immediately and was prepared to pay any price. When Shri. Dutt asked him why he wanted them, he replied, "I had sent a patrol to search a reported hideout of the hostiles." They succeeded in capturing documents, some equipment, and a bayonet. The hostile Nagas escaped in the dark. I sent a report, but there came a reply that during the last fifteen days, none of the patrols of my unit had been successful in capturing any arms, which would subsequently affect the good name of my unit and the formation I was under.

The incident was fresh in my memory. I looked at Mehta. My conscience pricks me night and day for having signed so many false documents. Often I weep over it in despair."

He wiped tears from his eyes. "I have tried to advise him, but he says that he knows much more about the Nagas than I do. Having heard that the officer is amorous, the notorious hostile leader from our area encouraged his sister, who stays in the village, to be intimate with the officer, and she succeeded. Even though I require a pass to enter the protected area, she can enter any quarter at any hour of the day or night without being questioned. Relief, rations, and clothes are kept for safe storage with the officer. Fifty percent of it has been taken away by her for her family and brother, who is hostile to the government and his followers."

I reported the matter to the higher authorities, who in turn warned him. The result was that I came in for more trouble and was even threatened with death. Encouraged, the girl opened a comfort center in the camp for the officers who take leave for a day or 2 and come for a visit here. A few days earlier, the account of relief distribution was to be submitted. When I asked the officer how to account for the shortage, he made me sign expenditure vouchers at the point of the gun and submitted those."

He shuddered with fear, which overpowered his nerves again. He was cold. "I am the only witness to all this. Even if I do not speak and reveal it to anyone, I will be murdered by my people. I deserve it! I deserve it! I have committed many sins." Seeing that he was about to collapse, with the help of my staff, I warmed him and put him to bed in the adjoining room.

The whole night, I meditated on the problem. The hostile lender in question was a dangerous man. He had fired the first shot when the hostilities began and murdered Late Shri T. Sakhrie, the most intellectual and trusted follower of Phizo, who opposed any violent activities and joined the group opposed to Phizo. His kin had said that he could exploit anyone for anything and would not hesitate to kill his parents for his benefit. But how could other people behave like him was the question!

I tried my level best to persuade Mehta to leave the place, but he declined. Luckily, the officer left the area soon. I persuaded the authorities concerned to appoint Mehta to a government job and transfer him to a distant place, but it was too late. He went to shikar with one of his friends early in the morning and would have returned before dusk, but on his way back, a few hostile Nagas requested him to come for a discussion. He entered the outskirts of the village just after dusk, where there were 10 to fifteen huts. Some unknown persons assaulted him, and a struggle developed. His companion escaped and rushed to the camp of the security forces, but before he returned, Mehta was shot. He expired on the way.

Not much later, the hostile leader surrendered for medical treatment and was placed in the officers' ward. The miscreants who killed Mehta remain untried and unpunished. Probably, they are flourishing, whereas a genuine worker paid with his life so that a lie might remain on record as truth forever.

Mahatma Gandhi survived and triumphed while experimenting with the truth. Can others also either succeed or at least survive?

30

A MATTER OF JEALOUSY!

Never were there complaints against the subordinate officers of my department at the outposts. They had earned the affection and respect of the locals due to their initiative, zeal, missionary attitude, and trustworthiness. All, irrespective of rank, worked with a spirit of dedication to the national cause. They had merged themselves with the locals in every way. If one of them was transferred for administrative reasons, locals shed tears and not only petitioned but came to Kohima to request his detention.

Some were experienced hands with a long service record, but the majority were those commissioned into service very recently. They came from all the states in India - Assam, Orissa, Bihar, Bengal, U.P., Punjab, Maharashtra, Gujarat, Madras, and Kerala. None complained about the place of posting, be it in the interior or a far-off jungle, coupled with unsuitable accommodation, shortage of amenities, and difficulty in getting food. Even when the General Officer Commanding, in his temperamental style, once stopped the supply of food and rations to them without any notice, they remained at the post enduring all the difficulties for over 7 days and carrying out the work in a normal way.

I always felt proud of the boys and their mental outlook. They were neither trained for the special task and the circumstances nor had they undergone courses and cadres to know what was happening or the psychology of the locals. All the background they had before they went to the outpost to take charge was a six-week stay in Kohima, during which period they worked with me.

On seeing that they not only merged with the people so quickly and worked with such devotion and zeal, but I also used to wonder why officers of other services could not feel and act likewise and why it was essential to start a special cadre named the Indian Frontier Administrative Service exclusively for the frontier areas!

Once, when the first phase of disturbances was over and the situation had eased, I received complaints against one of my officers at an important outpost. The complaints were not from the people but from a senior officer of another service. I knew my officer well as he had worked with me for over a year in a most difficult period. I sent a team to inquire and was satisfied with their report that it was a question of personal jealousy. Therefore, I decided to ignore the complaint, but the matter did not end there. The complaints were routed through higher channels with a demand for his immediate removal from the post.

Given the extremely good work done by the officer and his vast contacts, I was not prepared to transfer him. Ultimately, I went to investigate. None, not even a child, complained against him from among the locals. All officers of all the services, except the complainant, his staff officer, and one of the Naga officers, did not complain against him but praised him for his efficiency, devotion to duty, and excellent behavior. The complainant admitted that he did good work but complained about his behavior with locals. I was amazed at the allegation and asked him why the locals did not complain against him. Promptly, he replied that they were afraid to protest. I could not accept it as sound reasoning, for Nagas had never hesitated to complain against the highest authority for even the loss of a few trees.

Late in the evening, I went to the house of the Naga officer who had supported the complainant, as he was my friend. I asked him, over a glass of wine, to give me the background of the complainant. He roared with laughter. Placing his hand on my shoulder, he said, "Forget all about it. He is a good officer. There is nothing wrong with him."

"But you supported the complainant. You are aware that it affects the career of the officer, the reputation of my department and myself, and the prestige of the services. You are an elder to me. Not only do I respect you but also look up to you for guidance and help. You must help in solving this problem. There is a continuous demand for his removal from here."

"I had to support the complainant. Our promotions are due. Our senior officers will ask the complainant for a report on me, and until a report is submitted, I have no alternative but to support him in whatever he says. Take no notice of it. There is no truth in it. I wanted to meet you privately and tell you all about it, but he kept me engaged until late hours hoping that I could not meet you. Take no notice of it and forget it." I persisted, "I must know the origin and reasons for the complaint."

"The trouble is that your officer is young and handsome," he said laughingly. "I wish I had his personality when I was young. I would not have married till I was in my forties. All this trouble has been caused by a pretty girl. The senior officer spotted her and provided her with a new house and all the luxuries so that he could have her as a companion as long as he stayed in the station. But she does not care for him. According to her, he is old and ugly. She is after your officer. Once she got so enraged with him openly that she said she was in love with your officer and could marry nobody else. This incident originated the complaint. He feels that if your officer is removed from this station, he will have no rival, and she will yield to his desires. Your officer too is an idiot. He has some high ideals and principles, and so he does not care for the girl at all, though she feels that she will allure him finally."

He came very close to me and said in a whispering voice, "My neighbor's daughters are also after your officer, and we find it very difficult to control them. Whenever he comes to me for work in the morning, my neighbor's daughters miss their schools to get an opportunity to talk to him."

After he had once again assured me that there was no truth in the complaint and that I should not worry about it, I left. But with the cat out of the bag, I knew the real reason why he too had supported the complainant. It was the behavior of the 2 daughters of his neighbor.

I met with other officers and then with the girl in question, and the origin of the complaint was confirmed by everyone. The young officers pitied the complainant, who was an old phony for considering himself to be Romeo even though married. One officer confided that only a few days earlier he had been severely reprimanded by the complainant for making advances to the girl in question and had been given a sermon on good behavior as they were out on a special mission in Naga Hills.

On my return to Kohima, I thought over the problem but could not come to any conclusion to solve it in any other way than to transfer my officer from there. Not only did it mean a loss of prestige but acceptance of the complaint as true. In the end, I decided to forego the point of prestige in the interest of the services. I transferred the officer to remove any friction after having made known to the higher authorities the origin of the complaint.

It did not stop there. The complaints were renewed against the newcomer from my department. It was done to prove that the previous ones were true. A lie once spoken had to be adhered to, and I could not transfer him. Ultimately, I persuaded a handsome Naga boy to go to the place and take the girl out for himself. I paid all his expenses, and he did the job, leaving no rivalry or cause for complaint. Meanwhile, the newcomer from my department brought his wife to stay with him to remove any doubts about himself.

I had never imagined that just a girl could cause so much worry for my staff and myself and open a rift between officers of different services.

31

THE 'BIRTH' PROBLEMS OF A NEW CADRE IN NAGALAND

A few of the Naga officers who were earlier members of the Assam Provincial Service came to my office with a newspaper in hand. They had hopes of joining the IAS, and now they were members of the I.F.A.S. (Indian Frontier Administrative Service), a new cadre created after Naga Hills and Tuensang Area were carved out of Assam and NEFA (Northeast Frontier Agency), subsequently named **Nagaland**.

As they sat down, one of them showed me a news item. I had read it earlier. It was an appeal issued by Shri. Govind Vallabh Pant, the Union Minister, addressing all Government servants to work with missionary zeal and devotion so that not only would the living conditions of the people be improved but the newly achieved independence would be consolidated. I told them that every government servant should give it a thought, and I had already sent copies of it to the officers of my department posted in Naga Hills, suggesting it be carefully studied and to change their outlook accordingly.

"Officers of your department need no further coaching on the subject," said one of them. "Under your guidance, they have already surpassed a missionary in service to the people and the nation. You and your staff have earned more popularity among the Naga than any Indian since the departure of the British. But yours is not an administrative service. We must administer them. We are the custodians of law, order, and the well-being of the people. How can we combine the 2 facts, that we should consider ourselves as servants of the people and at the same time be superior to administer them? Furthermore, we must safeguard the prestige and dignity of the service, the officer class, and the nation. We have many other problems in the service, so we thought we might come to you for an informal discussion."

"It may be better for you to approach the senior-most officer from your service for that purpose," I suggested. "On previous occasions, we have done so," one of them replied. "We do not want lectures. What we want is a free and frank discussion so that we may be convinced. Unless we are convinced of the cause, how can we bring it into practice?" I could understand their puzzled attitude. They were not the only ones who had this dilemma. Many others were wanting to find their way and make their careers successful. But they probed in darkness due to the lack of set rules and regulations, guidance, and training at different stages throughout their careers, unlike those in vogue in the armed forces.

The essentials needed for one to build up a career, as well as to make a good administrator, could be summarized as follows: direct contact with the seniors and personal guidance from them day-to-day in the office, in the field, and in the mess, which brings about a team spirit and infuses loyalty to the superiors and the nation. In addition, continuous training in different subjects an officer must handle, at different stages of a career, through the means of courses, cadres, and exercises as is in practice in the armed forces. However, these are absent in the civil services.

Once trained and qualified, the contact between the newly appointed I.A.S., I.P.S., or I.F.A.S., or any other All-India or provincial service officer with seniors, even though working in the same office, is more on paper through notes and minutes. As a result, the newly appointed, inexperienced officers are left in the dark as to when to use their initiative to deal with unforeseen problems! As new problems crop up daily, in the absence of any training and guidance to deal with these, the new baby is left in the lurch, to be blamed afterward. As always, the man on the spot is held responsible. The civil services are required to deal with complicated problems and issues compared to their armed brother officers. Furthermore, they must maintain a positive relationship with politicians from the ruling party. It is the Minister in charge of the Home Department who has the final authority for transfer and promotion. The Minister may give more weight to what his party members say about an officer rather than his confidential records and the report of his departmental chief. Hence, regardless of how capable and strong his chief may be, the subordinate's loyalty and actions are divided and motivated as he is compelled to keep an eye on the politician on the spot and earn a good report from him.

The chief criterion for promotion is the confidential reports and the goodwill and reports of local politicians belonging to the ruling party. An officer does not have the right to question any adverse remarks in the confidential reports. It is taken for granted by practice that a senior officer has the right to express any opinion about the ability and characteristics of an officer under him, and it is unchallengeable. Unlike in the armed forces, the confidential reports are not shown to the person who is being reported on!

The problems that civil service officers must deal with are new and varied every day, yet there is no procedure in place to train them to handle these issues. I often felt that a newly appointed officer to the civil services was like a carved idol in any temple. If he fails to draw the attention of worshippers, he perishes and becomes a stepping-stone for someone else. If he succeeds, then he is garlanded and promoted to a higher position. In the absence of further training, guidance, and personal contact, all that is ideal for a newly appointed officer are the examples set by senior officers, resulting in administrators with distinctive characteristics, ideas, traditions, and customs forming a chain in the same line and cadre. All these difficulties often make him shy of direct contact with the masses, creating an external desire to try to get a posting in the secretariat so that he can find solace there in the files.

There was a greater need for the officers of the civil services to attend cadre's new courses, refresher courses, and exercises to deal with the increasing problems, more than those in the armed forces so that the administration became a thorough affair and not an experimental arena. The conferences and seminars held so often were restricted to academic discussions only, ending in dinners and cultural shows. While my reading of the situation had some merit, I also knew that very good and able persons were at the helm of each regime and knew better what was required. I first thought I would suggest to my visitors that I was not competent enough, either to solve their problems and doubts or to advise them, even after our discussions with workable solutions! However, I decided to continue so that I could learn and discover more about their problems. I asked them to enlighten me as to why they felt that the appeal in question by the home minister and their ideas of prestige and dignity of service clashed.

"Up to now, we were not conscious of the prestige of the officer class and the service," one of them said. "Since we are part of the IFS cadre, we shoulder a very heavy responsibility in that respect." "What has increased the responsibility overnight?" I asked them. They replied, "Now we belong to the IFS service of the specially selected intellectuals, who possess the dominating personality of the Himalayas, the integrity of Ashoka, and those who are prepared to dedicate and sacrifice their lives for the nation. Only the cream of other services is accepted into it." "On us lies the responsibility of being custodians of law and order on the difficult frontiers of India. We also bear a burden of transmitting the fame of India for efficient administration across the border." He paused a bit and then continued, "We must digest and apply special psychology when working. We must possess special stamina and be prepared to work 24 hours a day. We must consider work as recreation and vice versa. When in Rome, we must behave as Romans do and dress alike."

"I don't see you wearing Naga clothes," I observed. They replied, "Things differ for each area; in the Naga hills, Naga officers prefer to use Western dress. At present, as a first step, Officers' wives must use the Naga shawl while going out. I think we will restrict it to that forever, anyway, it is a service of specialized individuals. We look to only our superiors for a good report. We are free from the domination of politicians, and we do not have to deal with them at any stage. We must ensure that the people we administer are not exploited by the advanced people of other states and that the traditional customs and artful dress of the citizens of the frontier area are maintained." The speaker was excited and felt immensely proud.

"I agree with what you have said; these are indeed good ideas," I answered calmly. Encouraged, he continued, "This cadre to administer the frontier areas was specially formed, as it is noticed that its incumbents are unable to cope and deal with the situation, with no dedication to the cause. We are told that after a careful study of the chaos created in other states which are administered by other services, as compared to the efficiency in the area administered by our cadre, not only is the existence of a cadre justified but sooner or later our cadre must replace officers of other services in other disturbed states and restore normalcy and efficiency."

"Who told you this?" I asked in a perturbed mood, as I had never expected such thoughts to be instilled in the minds of newly appointed officers to the cadre. Anyway, it was not going to help to get emotional, as national integration, which is so essential after the formation of linguistic states, had developed separate tendencies. "We have had a few lectures on the subject, and you can experience it here!" he said proudly. "You can see the chaos caused in Naga Hills by the officers and other services since 1947." The first Indian deputy commissioner, after the British left, was Rev. Sipple, head of the mission at Kohima."

"It is only to cover their lapses that all of them have been replaced by officers of the IFS cadre. Only the other day a chief when lecturing the people of the Lotha area told them that as soon as they realized the difference between the administrations across the border and within, as now they had selected officers to look after Naga Hills, it would get better. So, you can well imagine what heavy responsibility is to be shouldered. Only a few months earlier when we belonged to the Assam Provincial Services, we were no one. Now we feel as if we are all mighty. Each of us has a jeep. We must be with people and yet far off, to save and guard our prestige and make the people feel our presence in person when we are in the station and spirit when we are absent from it."

"I have understood all the qualifications required to be in the IFAS and requirements of an officer, but where do you differ from the appeal of the home minister?" I questioned him to bring him to the point. This appeal is by the home minister, and we work under the Ministry of External Affairs, which is headed by the Prime Minister. The appeal may be directed to the other services and not those of the IFAS cadre. These days if you see the officers of other cadres, one wonders whether the essential quality of personality has been deleted from the requirements. Previously, officers of the services were tall with the dominating personality, whose presence could be felt from a distance, but nowadays hardly anyone exceeds 5 and a half feet. If they go anywhere in the crowd, they are liable to get lost." His vendetta against the other services continued. "It is the result of the invention that, where there is an intellectual brain, the growth of the human being is small and where the growth is dominant, the brain is of lesser prominence."

"But you have not touched upon the subject of difference." To cut short his line of thought, I once again reminded him of this. Turning to one of his companions, I asked, "At least you can touch the subject you came here for?" "Yes, Sir," he said with an air of elevated personage. The difference between the appeal and our attitude is that if we adopt the austerity of missionaries, their zeal and initiative to go from door to door, to inquire about the well-being of the people, the people will treat us as if we are beggars. Furthermore, then often when carrying out government orders, we must admonish and punish them, hence we must be away and above to administer and bring them prosperity. We cannot be servants of the people as well as superiors to them as administrators."

I replied, "I do not think the appeal in question asks any servant of the state to lower his position to that of a beggar while serving the people. We are servants of the state which belongs to the people. The state is governed by the body elected by the people; they decide on policies in consultation with people's representatives in the legislatures on what they assess as good for the people. The servants of the state are responsible for ensuring that it is understood properly, interpreted, and executed. Hence, collectively and individually, the officers of the district level are the real administrators to safeguard the interest of the state and the people. Every officer above the level of the district officer is only a link to the staff between the policymakers and the real administrators who are in contact with the masses and have only supervisory responsibilities. You can easily compare it with the army where there are only 2 real commanders, e.g., the battalion commander and the chief of army staff. All other high-ranking officers of the rank from Colonel to Lt. General are nothing but staff officers who rarely meet the troops."

As usual with them, Nagas listened patiently. I continued, "Probably the reason for the appeal could be found in the basic difference between the outlook of the armed forces and the civil services. First, an officer will consider the task of handling the well-being and comfort of his men and then that of himself, either in the form of residential or office at the foundation level. In the latter, an officer will first think of himself, residential accommodation for himself and his family, and a dignified place to start his office before he even thinks of the people and task at hand. Indeed, one deals with well-disciplined forces and the other semi-disciplined men, and undisciplined masses, but the basis of difference in the outlook remains the same. In addition, the former is willing to mix with people under him, play, and eat with them resulting in his being respected by the men through affection and love. Thus, he is not shy of the masses. The latter tries to get respected by remaining excluded and inaccessible."

Having offered them cigarettes, I lit one for myself. "It is incorrect to think that the missionary loses dignity and prestige. He is far above others in his conduct and his outlook. Not only does he remain clearheaded, but he also makes the people respect and acknowledge him as such because of his human approach, understanding of others, help to the needy and those suffering, and by his approach. He takes them nearer to God amidst worldly temptations and sufferings. In short, he safeguards the Kingdom of God by looking after the interests of the people. First off, once one becomes an officer at a level and derives some privileges and rights even to punish a man. If one uses it to safeguard his prestige on the basis and argument that he must be respected for it, then he has failed in his duty. If an officer thinks deeply and places himself as a minister of God, then probably the thought of prestige, dignity, and seclusion from the masses will not touch his mind. Not only will the interests of the state remain safe in his hands, but he will be loved, admired, and respected even more."

"A few minutes earlier, you paid compliments to my officers and said that they had surpassed the missionaries. Have they lost respect, dignity, and prestige? On the contrary, they receive more affection, admiration, and respect. Indeed, some officers of other services look down upon them, but it is due to jealousy, to safeguard their interests. It is a false belief that if one looks down upon others, one is superior to them. Also, one of you a few moments earlier condemned all other services to justify and visualize that you belong to the only service that is worth retention. We can talk on the subject for hours, but all that I would say is that you should study the appeal carefully, and you will find the key to your success. Here you are concerned only with a single line of administration, but in other parts of India, there is a cry for decentralization of the administration and establishment of a Panchayat Raj so that people can have a real say in the administration. It can be successful if the administrators at their district and lower levels follow the appeal by maintaining efficiency and not conduct themselves as a governor with protocols and no effective executive interest and responsibility."

"Then why should our seniors lead us the wrong way?" asks one of them. "I do not think anyone does it intentionally. It is the result of egoism and anxiety to prove that one is right and prove one is worth, with promotion and prosperity in mind," I said. "Probably I am not conversant with the line of thought of administrators, but if such differences have reached and echoed, it will increase separatist tendencies and not help the integration of the nation." "I think we have spent a lot of time probably and you have work. At least I certainly must deal with some work, as so many visitors are waiting outside. If you still desire, we will continue the discussion some other day." They left, and I devoted myself to other visitors and work. I had not expected them to come back again. But they did come a week later when they declared their intention to continue the discussion. I told them to be precise and concrete and asked them how they happened to come to Kohima so often.

"Since we met you last, we have not returned to our posts," one of them explained. "We have truly little to do at the post; the work is nothing but a repetition, and the place has no recreational facilities. Further, we have come to Kohima so often to consult higher authorities for advice and decisions. So, it is better to remain here. You are right; when we were in Shillong, we saw that not only the commissioner in charge of the plains division but engineers, forest and transport officers, and those of education and other departments, those connected with the plains areas come and stay in Shillong so that they can have better and easier contact with higher authorities. Even though they are of Northeast Frontier Agency and Shillong is miles and miles away from any NEFA. I asked them the reason for being so far away from the place of work, and he told me that these days, it is more important to be in contact with and in service to the higher officers in the interest of service and promotion than to be with the people concerned on the spot. People can wait indefinitely, but higher authorities and the government cannot wait for any delay in reply or submission of a report.

Again, it was a case of procedures set up by the senior officer to be complied with and acted upon by the juniors. I could not question or contradict them as they were justified in presuming that they were right in the procedure they followed. "There is another aspect to it," said one of the younger officers. "I was told by an officer that he could not move to the place of work as the center of jurisdiction has no suitable residential and office accommodation available there for himself and his staff till it is built. It could be in either the second or 3rd plan. He would consider shifting there, but then he may be transferred or promoted to another post in Shillong. We have no suitable accommodation to work in comfort and in a dignified way. Unless we have peace of mind, how can we all achieve work? Similar conditions prevail in the NEFA setup."

He was correct, but I thought of many formations of headquarters of the armed forces which even now survived in tents and huts all over India. Officers too worked separately from families without losing dignity, prestige, comfort, and peace of mind. To avoid further delay, I requested them to state the purpose of the visit.

"During the last few years, we have received many instructions formally and informally. The foremost point worrying us is about corruption. Why should it ever occur and how can we prevent it? We understand it is rampant at all levels, that half of the money meant for the plans is misappropriated." This came from one of the officers. I could notice that he seemed worried. "I cannot support and confirm that half of the money is misappropriated, for I do not know about it. I will tell you how to avoid it. Do you agree that many more capable and intelligent youths like you have not been lucky to be appointed as officers in any cadre?" "Yes, I do agree," he promptly answered. "Some of them flourish in business while others must remain content as teachers and clerks somewhere."

I asked him to consider their fate and finances. "You are luckier. As an officer, you will enjoy a decent living and many other facilities! It is good to be content with what you earn, and specifically make your wife understand it and live within your means. If you do it, you will never be guilty, with your conscience clear, you will lead a happy life with your head held high. More often than not, an officer starts misappropriation or is forced by circumstances created at home. Competing with those who are more fortunate creates needs and increases domestic expenditure beyond a husband's means. Whenever such an officer has a personal need or a ceremony to attend, he undertakes an official tour of the place, attends to his work, and returns to headquarters. There are some exceptions to it, and such people are those who have cut off all connection with their kith/kin and are content to live with their families, needing no leave to attend anything.

"To keep happiness in the house, he tries to get the required money by other means and goes astray. Not all who go astray are likely to be punished. One who adopts the method of letting everyone be dishonest and happy by any means never complains. One who only looks after his benefit and denies it to others is exposed and punished."

32

POLITICS PLAYED BY ADMINISTRATORS, LEARNING TO DEAL WITH VIP'S

"There is one more very delicate point," said the youngest, "if you promise not to mention it to anyone else, we will open this subject." I assured them, and he slowly started. "Nowadays we are facing great difficulty due to the rift between the Commissioner and the Deputy Commissioner. They do not agree. The result is that we are in a very embarrassing position."

This subject was not new to me as I had heard of it personally from officers concerned with top-ranking political leaders. Both officers were of excellent mettle with many virtues in them. The conflict was due to the egoism of one and the firm conviction and ideology of the other. Indeed, it was a shameful thing that instead of ironing out differences privately or officially, these are being made public to oust one another.

To safeguard the prestige of the officer concerned, I asked them not to worry. Such things do occur but will disappear. If they have gone far in their differences, they are seeking the support of the officers and the political leaders to prove to the higher authorities that they are supported by both. "Oh!" the officer exclaimed. "What you have said appears to be a reasonable answer."

I was surprised as another elderly officer said, "Even the armed forces are taking part and supporting the commissioner. We have seen differences between officers but not the kind we experience here. The present conflict has taken the shape of a ruling political party with dissidents in it. Both are trying to seek popular support. Is it permitted in the government servants' conduct rules?"

"The other day, the select committee of the Naga People's Convention also held a meeting to discuss the subject. The president said they should be united in demanding that either the officers work amicably as a team for the betterment of the Nagas or both go. If we go to the commissioner, he asks why we have come to him. We should meet the deputy commissioner and take instructions. But sometimes, he sends for us and says that to keep up the efficiency of the administration, he must take a shortcut and give instructions. He also asked what we thought of the deputy commissioner. How can we say something against our immediate boss? Are such methods practiced in other parts of India also?"

There is another point the eldest among them said. "Recently, I have asked for leave. Before I joined the present cadre, whenever I asked for leave from my superior officer, he got annoyed. He told me that during the last 3 years, he has not taken leave for even a day, quoting examples of many who had not taken leave for 10 years. I wondered how it could be. Do they not have domestic or personal problems? Do they not need rest, or have they no kin and kin whom they would like to meet? I feel lost when I think about it. I am told that in the armed forces, you get 60 days of leave every year, and even when in an emergency, you are allowed to avail of it."

I replied, "Sometimes leave is stopped in an emergency, but such occasions are rare. Officers are encouraged to take leave as it cannot be accumulated, whereas in civil services it can be accumulated up to a certain limit and it can be availed of even after retirement." After clarifying the position, I went on, "If I am not wrong, the system originated when British officers served in India and could not afford the journey to their homes every year, but they did visit their homes every 2 to 3 years. Even today, similar conditions prevail as officers from one corner of India serve at the other end. So, if anyone has not taken earned leave for 2 to 3 years, it is understandable, but you will find that those who boast they have not taken leave for a period more than that are those who serve in their home state and can tour the whole of the state. Their needs are the same as those of others and under the garb of a tour, they visit the place where they have private work."

"Provision of leave has been made after careful study of the needs of human beings and the psychological effects. An officer who does not take leave for more than 3 years may be considered as getting all the entertainment assured he needs after normal office work. It would be better if you ask someone who has not taken leave for many years how to do it. Whatever it is, I want to take leave every year. I must have some change from the routine office work."

As an officer, I felt embarrassed that even newly appointed officers should discuss such a subject at the beginning of their career. They will carry an everlasting impression of it and practice similar tactics to oust rivals in the service.

A few days earlier, Dr. Imkongliba Ao, the president of the Naga People's Convention, had come to me concerning this. He said it is a pity that the government cannot send mature officers who have no ax to grind. If you study the history of the administration here since 1947, you will find that probably except for Shri SJD Carvalho IAS, every other administrator had to quit for some reason or another. Everyone starts experimenting and does not apply policies with a firm hand. I have talked to the general officer commandant of the security forces. He likes neither of them nor said that if one goes today, the other will follow him eventually. Better tell the Prime Minister to send selected officers of standing and not every Tom, Dick, and Harry to experiment, quarrel with each other, and wash dirty linen in public. Both should quit immediately.

I remembered the lecture I had heard on "Yad" about the unknown grave at Kohima. Wise men had precisely summarized some important subjects faced by the people in government service. I wanted to discourage the youngsters from discussing this further, at least in my presence. In the past, people had clamored for the removal of administrators. Here was an example of administrators seeking the support of the masses to remove one another.

"To tell you the truth, what is happening is a sad episode," I said to the young officers, "you will agree that human beings differ from one another and have different personalities. Everyone has virtues, defects, and shortcomings. As an officer, it is a duty to ensure that personalities do not conflict and that virtues are pooled to build up a team spirit in the interest of the nation. If you follow the appeal of the home minister and put to the forefront the essential points mentioned therein, of the interest and well-being of the people, personal ambitions, egoism, likes, dislikes, and conflicts between personalities will be buried in the background, giving a fillip to a team spirit, so essential for emotional integration and for which we have been appointed as servants of the state. If one fails, then in fact, there is no greater enemy of the state than us." The young officers were in a mood for discussion, but I was not as I had to go to a meeting, and so we parted.

The senior officer must have their say, so the deputy commissioner left first, but soon thereafter the commissioner left overnight due to a conflict between personalities higher than themselves.

The stormy monsoon weather was over, and cold winds were blowing across the sky. The hill, which appeared fascinating during the day and adorned the peaks with crimson curves during sunset, became massive, formidable blocks under an umbrella of blue sky and twinkling stars after dusk. The villagers, who enjoyed greater freedom due to lesser destructive activities of the hostile Nagas, were happy at the prospect of a good harvest. They were busy repairing and retouching their huts and grain stores on the outskirts of the villages. The schools functioned without any interference from the hostiles. Everyone agreed that along with the weather, the situation had taken a turn for the better.

The monotony of the routine was broken by the news that a semi-VIP (especially important personality) from Delhi was to visit Kohima. It had caused excitement in the official circle, and brisk preparations were in effect to impress him with the progress made and the capabilities of the officers in charge and to prove that all reports sent regarding the progress were correct.

If the visitor is accompanied by his wife, then the plight of the Hostess is difficult. The Hostess not only has to draw up a separate program to keep the wife occupied and arrange social welfare shows and meetings but cannot devote all her attention to the VIP who would draft the confidential report on her husband. She does not take liberties with the visitor for fear of annoying his better half accompanying him. In this case, the visitor was coming unaccompanied by his wife, leaving the Hostess and wives of the officers with time to devote all their skill, time, and tact in conversation to humor him so that he is pleased, and they cherished the aim of enhancing the position of the officers concerned.

Starting with the reception at Dimapur and a welcome address at the civic body, which consisted of contractors and illegal migrants from Pakistan, everything went off smoothly as pre-arranged, till the item of a public reception at the panchayat hall in Kohima. A welcome address was designed so that at least over one thousand persons could be inside, and other thousands were present outside. To achieve this, many steps were taken. The chief priest announced "Ghena," forbidding people from leaving the village, and a community feast was to be held after the reception for about 2 thousand villagers who participated.

The panchayat hall was semi-full, but it was not going to have the desired effect. Many men, women, and children who indeed wanted to attend were obstructed from doing so by the hostiles at the point of a gun and stood at a distance unable to make their way forward. It is not feasible to use arms against the Nagas, as armed conflict would have led to the cancellation of the reception. A few minutes were left for the VIP to come, and whose cavalcade was seen ready at the residence of the commissioner. Under pressure from the people, the hostiles agreed to allow them to join the gathering, provided the officers removed the Indian national flag. Nagas who were in the panchayat hall opposed it. In their eagerness to fulfill the desires of their master and impress the visitors, officers in consultation with the host concerned agreed and unfurled (?) the national flag.

The reception was very impressive indeed, and the VIP returned immensely impressed. Individuals gained at the cost of the state. Personal gain is material in this world. For many the state is spiritual, for which many others have sacrificed, some are sacrificing, and will sacrifice their lives at the call and preaching of the leaders. Unmindful of material gain and individual prosperity.

I remember a true story told by a friend. An immensely popular leader was visiting the capital of a state. The sight of crowds waiting en route to greet him and take his darshan gave him the highest pleasure. Due to some emergency, the leader decided to leave by the next available train which was at 2:00 a.m., and it was unlikely that people would turn up at that hour. The Inspector General of Police, a resourceful man, assured that the need would be fulfilled. He collected men of his district executive force, not on duty, those of armed units, and army units, plus many wives and children of the forces. He transported them to important points dressed as civilians. The visitor returned overly impressed with his popularity and that of his party in the state, with people gathered at such an hour to greet him even though he had decided to leave on short notice.

33

MISSING MAHATMA GANDHI

"Life had ebbed from the immortal soul of Mahatma Gandhi, the father of the nation, but the flame he kindled lights every corner of India and will continue to do so forever." "Naga Hills is not an exception to it," said Visar Angami, a veteran who believed in the ideologies and teachings of Mahatma Gandhi and practiced them.

He was there to complain that he had lost his book The Experiments with Truth by the Mahatma. "I feel lost without the book. I have always carried it with me and even kept it under my head when I slept elsewhere. I am without the book, but my memory and my notes will not fail me. Pandit Nehru's grief on hearing the news is something worth remembering." Opening his notebook, Visar read out, "The spirit has gone out of our lives and there is darkness everywhere, and I do not know quite what to tell you, and how to say it. Our beloved leader Bapu is no more. You will never see him again as we have seen him for these many years. We will not run to him for advice and seek solace from him."

"'The light has gone,' I said, and yet I was wrong. The light that shone in this country was no ordinary light. The light has illuminated this country for so many years, will illuminate it for many more years, and one thousand years later, that light will be seen in the entire world, and it will give solace to innumerable hearts. For that light represented the living truth, the eternal man was with us with his eternal truth reminding us of the right path. Drawing us from error, leading the ancient country to freedom."

He closed his notebook and placed it in his haversack, continuing to speak with his usual smile. "There are so many Nagas who not only had the honor and pleasure of staying with Mahatma Gandhi but also underwent training as gram sevaks at Sevagram. But where are they today? Ignored and forgotten in these days of dominance of politics and religion, cold and hot war egoism, and personal uplift, they have become lifeless."

"For those still on this Earth now, it is a blunder to speak the truth. The right path has become a thorny one, and to point out an error is to invite calamity of insult and snubs. What the Mahatma preached has been reduced to mere written words, to be quoted at convenience, only for the guidance of others, and remembered only on the second of October. What he was appears today as something spiritual, and unless we go near it, we will not benefit from it. The facts to be remembered are that one requires the light when it is dark and solace when undergoing difficulties and mental torture. He realizes an error when ruined or defeated and reconciles to the right path thereafter, if any strength to encourage or to accept humiliation is left. The world is torn by the conflict of religion, politics, and armed conflict for material gain, and only salvation is in spiritualism."

"Have you visited the Gandhi ashram in Chunchuymland?" I said, "Not yet," though I had heard of it. "We will talk more on the subject after your visit," saying so, Visar left as suddenly as he had walked in. I had heard a great deal about the Gandhi ashram at Chunchuymland. It is the only institute that is non-official and non-Christian missionary in Naga Hills.

Shortly thereafter en route to Mokokchung, I visited the institute. The educational institute created in memory of Mahatma Gandhi was housed in a small building made from mud. Students, the majority of whom hailed from the Konyak and Sangtham areas, received training in literacy and handicraft work, to enable the boys to attain proficiency in a craft of their liking and lead an independent life as craftsmen and not go begging for clerical work.

Every effort was made to return and retain their traditional dress and other unique styles. Shri Thakkar, a young gentleman well-versed in Gandhian ideologies and who devoted his life to the service of the people, was at the head of the Institute along with local teachers who had volunteered to assist him. Shri Thakkar hailed from Bombay and had married an Ao girl who attired herself in Naga dresses or alternately in a sari, and was the symbol of emotional integration.

During the disturbances, they lived there unprotected and moved as such, despite the threats from some extremists in the hostile ranks and carefully declined protection by the security forces within the perimeter of the camp. Not demoralized by the plunder of the school property by the hostiles, he not only remained in his 2-room house nearby and worked with great zeal and determination.

He took me around the ashram and showed me a new building which was erected with the help of the students and craftsmen trained in the school. The youths spoke Hindi well and knew about Mahatma Gandhi and his teachings. The organizers were full of hope to make the institute a success and at the right time establish branches of the same in other areas.

Shri Thakkar explained briefly the problem in Naga Hills and the possible remedy to overcome it. He said the problem is one of emotional integration and it can be overcome if experienced officers take the cause in hand and work for and with the Nagas, instead of boasting that one has achieved it personally. Never discouraged by any difficulties, defeat, or humiliation, he however expressed sorrow at the apathy shown by the officials in Naga Hills toward the institute.

He said such a conflict arises out of immaturity and fear that if one visits the institute, takes interest in it and accords help, the critics on the land may allege inclination toward a partially foreign institute, the only one of Indian origin. The disinterest shown is due to the inability of the institute and the organizers to accept the ideas of officers as to how the affairs of the institute should be conducted and abided as per their guidelines. This could not be done, as theirs is an unofficial institute and will remain as such. Its systems cannot be changed every few years to follow the line of thought, and experiments made by the occupants of the official chair.

A few days later, I saw the truth behind what he said. The commissioner was to visit the institute during his return journey. Arches were put up by the students, and they lined up the route to the school. The organizers and locals were waiting to receive him. As the convoy of the commissioner approached and disappeared fast, Shri Thakkar ran after the commissioner's vehicle to remind him, but human legs could not compete with the mechanical acceleration. He returned with all dust over his face and body and told the students jokingly that the visitor would not come in, as he was too busy. While complexity and egoism rule at present, it will exit eventually. Officers will come and go, but the Institute raised in the memory of the great Mahatma will flourish forever.

A few days later, when Visar Angami with a few Goaburaha's visited my office, he casually asked what my impressions of the Gandhi ashram were. He heard the general picture I gave and said, "The building where the Institute is housed is unimpressive compared to the mission compounds in Naga Hills. I understand that it is a sign of austerity, but why make it applicable there when it is not applied anywhere else? I heard about the plight of the organizer when the much-publicized visit by the commissioner did not materialize due to pressure of other engagements."

"One of the teachers who came to solicit help said, the new administration has sanctioned the issue of free food to the borders in all schools, but the sanction excludes this institute. I went to the authorities concerned with him but failed to include this school. They said that the institute did not follow the curriculum issued by the government through the school board and hence the sanction could not be made applicable to it. There is much red tape everywhere. That was appalling!"

"As I said the other day, words of great men these days are quoted at convenience, as guidance for others. A few who follow such idealists never flourish. Here is an institute, if supported and with branches established all over, covering the educational and religious needs of the people, which will undoubtedly bring emotional integration through spiritualism and materialistic deeds."

Followers of Mahatma, whether Nagas or from any other state, could work to bring home to the masses, engulfed by material gain, to get the benefits of spiritual emancipation. And I heard that Dalai Lama said at a reception in Bomilla that he would not condemn this material world, as the gain and benefits from it relieved needy human beings, but spiritualism must not be forgotten, though it can only achieve some degree of happiness. The prospects of the Institute flourishing to help emotional and national integration were worth the thought. The people supported it and appreciated its aims and objectives and volunteered help, but it remained a neglected one."

"The main obstacle was the lack of support from the bureaucracy, and the reason for this was dislike for the institute all across. The organizer was disliked, as he worked under the guidance of a society, which controlled affairs of ashrams all over the country and did not take orders from the authorities on the spot. The organizer would write to and meet the highest authority in India, be it the president or the Prime Minister, without the knowledge and permission of the authorities on the spot. Express his views on the institution and the working of the administration, jeopardizing the efforts of the men on the spot to consolidate their positions, and thus hurt their vanity. He was a man to be feared. The institute was an eyesore, as its aim, object, and curriculum could not be changed, which were fixed by the rulers, the Gandhi society."

34

FOREIGN MISSIONS AND THE NEED TO TRAIN OFFICERS

"I wondered why no one criticized and interfered with the working of the foreign mission and the institutes operating under its patronage. Policy directions and funds for the mission were also received from outside Naga Hills. On the contrary, every effort was made to speak honorably about it and fraternize. I discussed it with my friends, officers of all shades of opinion, religion, and different services, thinking that one of them could lay his finger on the possible clue."

"The primary reason could be that the organizers of the missions have no direct approach to the President, Prime Minister, and superior officers as such. The fear that they may convey something contrary to that painted officially from here does not exist. If the missionaries write anything contradictory or damaging to their respective headquarters even abroad, the chances that it might reach the ears in Delhi are remote. The secondary reason is the overwhelming anxiety to maintain our state as a secular one. In Naga Hills, the mission's purpose is to spread Christianity and to safeguard the interests of those who are Christians and of the church. On the contrary, there is no institute and authority to protect the religion and interests of the Nagas who are not Christians."

"Hostile Nagas have already propagated falsely that Christianity is in danger. Anything said and done against the mission and its activities would find a place in the Press of the Western Hemisphere, which is Christian by faith. This would affect the claim of secularism, and one who utters and does anything different will face the wrath of the higher ones."

"Someone may term you to be a cynic," said one of the friends addressing the speaker. "So what? The duties and functions of officers are prescribed, and we have ceased to think freely or write after taking into consideration the pros and cons from all angles. Now we are expected to speak to suit the viewpoint of higher ones, and whenever one differs, he is claimed to be a cynic."

"The constitution guarantees freedom of speech and though I am in service, as a citizen, I claim my right. In our anxiety to safeguard the status of the secular state, many of us have begun to develop a complex. Especially, the Hindus shudder at the thought of visiting a place of worship of our faith in fear of losing popularity among those of other religions and being termed as communal. In our anxiety to appear secular in a secular country, many of us will not hesitate to ridicule our customs arising out of ignorance of religion. That is nothing but an inferiority complex and one will not find an example of it anywhere except in India." Saying so, he rose to

A valuable book, Philosophy for NEFA by Dr. Verrier Elwin, had become a Bible to every serving officer of the Northeast Frontier Agency. The book is educative. I read it out of curiosity and once again to understand the subject matter as advocated by the writer.

One of the young Naga officers had learned it by heart after his appointment as a circle officer. He was so very enthusiastic about it. He carried the book wherever he went and quoted passages from it in every conversation. It reminded one of a newlywed couple who carried photographs of one another and invariably praised one another in every conversation.

I had halted at his headquarters during the tour of my outpost. Throughout the day, he drew my attention to many paragraphs in the book and the foreword by Pundit Jawaharlal Nehru, Prime Minister of India. Late in the evening, as we were talking about it while having a drink, he pulled his chair near to me and said, "Sir, I want to ask you a question, provided you promise that you will never disclose it." I gave him the required assurance.

He took out the book, A Philosophy of NEFA, and pointing out the foreword and the preface asked, "Who got inspiration from whom? Both are reciprocal, how could it be?" Patting him on the back, I told him, "Do not worry and waste your time and energy in tackling the problem; it is called a protocol. How to observe and practice it is best known to individuals, especially important personalities." "But, Sir," he whispered, "It is a lesson to us."

"True! You are in your infancy in the official world, yet to earn and establish your reputation as an expert. It is not a bad idea to practice this art and compliment your seniors. It is too early to expect reciprocal compliments on par with those showered by you on your senior officers. For the time being, you must remain contented and consider yourself truly fortunate if your seniors say that you are a promising officer."

"I hope you understand and consider the difference between a newly appointed cook and a seasoned one, who has been in the company of the experts for a long time. Both may be equally proficient. The newly appointed cook, however good he may be at his work, could be easily accused of wasting food, spoiling it, being lazy, disloyal, and insubordinate. But once he understands his master's liking, line of thinking, and mood, with appropriate flattery, the young cook will be reciprocally complimented in public. Then he can afford to be arrogant, insubordinate, dishonest, lazy, and even serve spoiled food. His faults and sins will be merged with the philosophy of coexistence and protocol."

"If you want to be a successful officer these days, remember one thing: your senior in power is your master. Forget all your ideals and align your thinking to that of your master. Produce work to his liking to fit in suitably within the framework of his ideals. You will not only be honored and rewarded, but it could lead to a comfortable life."

"Anyway, tell me why you are so afraid to ask the question?" Pressing the book to his heart, he replied, "Sir, as a member of the Indian Frontier Administrative Service, it is a Bible for us. If I express any doubt or question a word of it, I may be exterminated in this single line of administration, like those who speak a word against the Bible in the church." I sympathized with him and said, "You will probably overcome it with your experience."

35

IS INDIA READY FOR ADULT FRANCHISE?

"Another important point: while military regimes in other countries are condemned by our politicians, it is being practiced in the Northeast Frontier Agency and Naga Hills, under the officers who once belonged to the services. We are free from interference from politicians and people. I and my senior officers are sure of success in establishing an ideal administration for a socialist state and setting an example for other states in India."

"Yet, I think that by national character, experience, and education, we are not fit for democracy based on adult franchise," I said. "There is probably much truth in what you say. However, it is not correct that all military regimes are criticized and condemned by politicians, as in powerful and friendly countries like Egypt."

Wishing good night, I retired to my room, which is not far away. Even though tired after the day's work, the words "even by our national character, experience, and education we are not yet fit for democracy based on adult franchise" rang in my ears. Could it be true or at least rational, I asked myself repeatedly!

Truly, we knew and practiced very little of parliamentary democracy. Full elections based on limited franchises, when introduced, were guided by officials and voters who exercised franchises as prompted and paid for.

When the Indian National Congress decided to contest elections in India, parliament, and provincial assemblies to achieve the goal of independence by constitutional means, people voted for any of its nominees unmindful of the nominee's popularity, leadership ability, and character, as long as the contestant adhered to the pledge of Mahatma Gandhi and worked hand in hand with the leaders of the movement to achieve the goal of independence.

Common people were more concerned with their daily needs of bread and butter and laboring hard to get through the environment of insurmountable economic difficulties. The thought of the future beyond the next day never occurred to them. The idea of independence and rebirth of nationality appealed more due to their inheritance, of personal connection with Mahatma Gandhi, the long-expected and long-prophesied acquisition of land that had belonged to the ancestors. Their devotion to the cause, no doubt, was due to the personal magnetism of Mahatma Gandhi, not that they understood either the political significance nor did the correctness of the reasoning convince them of the necessity to gain independence. They vaguely hoped that once India was free from foreign bondage, it would not be exploited under their own leaders' regime, also their deplorable economic state would improve, and they could march toward material prosperity. Mainly it was the personal magnetism of Mahatma coupled with the hope of material gain that made the masses leap into the struggle for independence.

History brutally unfolds an unpleasant factor against democracy in India. From time immemorial until the day the British quit India, the people have been accustomed to and owed allegiance to a national monarchy, which kept them united with the help of its force, administrators, and tact.

A strong monarchy always proved to be an antidote to discord and dissension. The moment the monarchy relaxed its control, feudalism revived, dividing the people and robbing the nationality of birthright. The people of India cannot discard their inherited outlook and tendencies overnight; they will continue to work for an old allegiance or a national hero, till they are educated to reason dispassionately and to pronounce judgment individually.

Neither has their cherished dream of a better life come fully true today, nor have they learned or been educated to exercise the franchise thoughtfully, after careful reasoning and considering the ideals of the political parties, the ability of the candidate, and what is good for themselves and who can deliver it best.

Though religion has now lost the influence it once exercised over politics, in the absence of education, which can result in dispassionate reasoning as to what is best for them, they still follow the cult of personality, a hereditary trend, which only the educated can understand. (!)

It is proved by the fact that when elections are held after 5 years, parties feel it is still essential not only to advertise the success achieved by the party but also the possible good that one can do if elected. This is done by taking out processions, holding meetings at which dancing allures the audience before addressing them, displaying placards and banners, distributing handbills, and disfiguring walls all over the cities, towns, and villages with scrawls that last till the next election. Not content with these, also threats, the use of violence, and criticism of other parties are adopted to scramble into power.

The normal courtesy observed by an advertiser of goods in commercial lines to spell out good about one's product, leaving it to the user to decide which is economical and best, is discarded by contestants, however high they may be placed in public life and esteem. They do not hesitate to wash others' dirty linen in public to prove their worth. All this is done by spending crores of rupees despite the outcry for national savings, and that too from the funds raised from the donations by the industrialist voters.

Despite all the propaganda and having been in power since the independence of India, to prove its worth, the Congress party had to count on the magic spell of Jawaharlal Nehru, a leader of international fame over the masses and make him undertake a whirlwind tour of constituencies in India. People who had blind faith in him, next to Mahatma Gandhi, could put the party into power. As someone said earlier, "Nehru is Congress and Congress is Nehru. Imagine independence without the personal magnetism of Mahatma Gandhi and the Congress without the personal magic spell of Nehru who is worshipped as a national hero."

Unfortunately, India has many religions and political divisions, the majority of which are based on personal aggrandizement resulting from hereditary feudalism, and which today have become a personality cult, of a lesser denomination than Congress. As a result, a strong opposition, which is essential for the smooth functioning of democracy so that the party in power and its leader do not assume a dictatorial role, cannot be achieved in India despite the overwhelming votes secured by the opposition parties combined in every election held since independence.

Defections and resignations from each party on the eve of the election and the fact that they readily find a place in another party indicate that except for the Communist Party, where resignations are few and not without purpose, political ideology and accreditation are flexible and arise out of convenience and personal gain.

The disproportionate and invalid votes, and percentage of those who do not vote, in each constituency, will undoubtedly support the fact that the voters need to be educated, for despite memorizing before entering the polling booth, they forget when facing the ballot box. No doubt even an advocate of coexistence and tolerance abroad of other ideologies like Pandit Jawaharlal Nehru seeing the attitude and standard of voters at home, emphasizes that the candidate whom he named as good must be accepted by the people.

He got irritated if either he or his stalwarts and his party were criticized on smaller issues, making it a matter of personal prestige! He could not see the reasoning behind or accommodate and tolerate any views contrary to his own, of patriots of equal standing who were not in his party. This was an attitude that resulted from the knowledge of personal magic spell over the masses and arrogance of power.

36

HOPES FOR AN IDEAL ELECTION AND THE REALITY!

Annual elections to the managing committee of the Shillong Club are still fresh in my memory. During the general meeting held to elect members to the managing committee, Shri Fakhruddin Ali Ahmed, a prominent Congress leader of Assam and the finance minister in the present cabinet, condemned the methods adopted by the contestants to canvas support. He advised them that once it had been made known that they were contesting elections, it is best to leave it to the members to decide who could serve them best by being on the committee.

Very practical and good advice, considering that the members of the club were highly educated and could appreciate and have a reason before giving judgment! They were not the illiterate masses of India who had blind faith and a pathetic faith in personality cults, whose minds were dominated by personal magnetism and magic.

However, once your candidate is elected, he forgets the voters and their dependence for 5 years. If in between they disapprove of his attitude and activities, and censor him, condemn his leadership, and demand his resignation, he is not bound by it unless the high command of the party approves of it. In a rare case, the party may give consent to the wish of the people and ask their individuals to resign for fear of losing the seat to the opposition in the face of the excitement and tense atmosphere in the constituency.

Presuming that the party executive approves and directs him to resign, he is not bound to obey, and it defies the wishes of the people. As the party executive, he can still sit in the opposition benches, where he is most welcome and retains the seat for the full tenure of 5 years. If such pathetic conditions prevailed in other parts of India, what would happen in NEFA and Naga hills where such elections were unheard of? Yet I console myself by saying that such conditions could contemporarily exist in India due to illiteracy.

Hence, people are educated and are not guided by personality cults and can see for themselves by cool and dispassionate reasoning and vote accordingly. To achieve it, we need a patriot who sees things clearly, not with a paralyzed vision from being in power for a long time, willing to work ceaselessly to educate the masses. We are sure to improve if, at the right time, the political divisions arising out of personal aggrandizement and heredity of blood feuds switch to the changing times!

To accept non-violent ways of dealing with the opposition parties, they should be narrowed down to 2 political parties so that we live peacefully in a real democracy and not be led in the direction of a communist or military totalitarianism, undermining the democratic way of life bestowed upon us by the constitution.

However, I wondered why no code of conduct was laid down for the contestants and those elected to represent the people. As some enthrone themselves as ministers. These people who supervise the work of the services could learn from the code of conduct and rules and regulations that are required to be followed by government servants.

But in reality, many such leaders, with their political somersaults and acrobatics during the election, could probably humor and entertain illiterate masses, and not the cream of intelligence here and in the country. They don't have to go far to search for good examples, avoid catastrophe, overcome the vacuum caused by national life based on real democracy, and achieve prosperity.

The chain of thought was unending. Sometime later, I fell asleep. When I woke up the next morning, I had forgotten the subject I pondered over so much during the previous night! At dawn, I was more concerned with the work I had to do during the day to earn my bread and butter.

Sometimes when thoughts creep up at night, I discard them, thinking that very recently wise men have succeeded in formulating a philosophy for Northeast Frontier Agency based on the ideals of Prime Minister Pandit Jawaharlal Nehru. And these ideals should help and guide the administrators and the would-be leaders! And with time, a clearer picture as to what is best for India would emerge, and these ideas could be then formulated and published.

"Naga Hills, a district of Assam, is now centrally administered as a newly created state. With no popular government coming up soon, we hope to attain the status of a full-fledged autonomous state. Yet the regulations restricting entry of non-Nagas must continue for an indefinite period to safeguard our interest," said one of the elderly Nagas during an informal discussion on necessary essential safeguards to prevent exploitation by advanced people.

By detaching the Naga Hills district from Assam and the Tuensang frontier division from the Northeast Frontier Agency, the new state of Naga Hills-Tuensang area, which was subsequently renamed Nagaland, was carved out, and yet the protection provided in the form of inner line regulations continued.

Protection of the underdeveloped areas in the hilly region around the border was accorded in the form of the Chin Hills Regulation, only known as Inner Line Regulations, from the days of British rule, to prevent exploitation of the indigenous people by citizens from more advanced parts and also preserve their religion, culture, traditions, customs, and let them lead a life in their way within these regulations. Non-residents of the area were not allowed entry within the area without a permit.

In the Northeast region, areas governed by these regulations fell under 3 district administrations. Districts of Lushai Hills, now Mizoram, and Mikir Hills were in Assam; Nagaland, a semi-autonomous state under the center, and then northeast frontier agency, now Arunachal, where single line administration existed and comprising the Kameng, Siang, Subansiri, Lohit, and Tirap frontier subdivisions, also came under the Ministry of External Affairs. Entry into districts of United Khasi and Jaintia Hills and Garo Hills, parts of Assam, was similarly restricted earlier, but the restrictions were withdrawn during the pre-independence times.

Foreign missionaries, however, were accorded access to the areas except the Northeast Frontier Agency, to establish educational and medical institutes. They had taken full advantage to convert the predominant portion of locals to Christianity. Also, the absence of organizations to protect the existing religion helped the conversion, partially defeating the very purpose of enforcing entry restrictions into these hilly areas.

These areas, even Assam itself, were unknown to people in the rest of India! However, post-independence, these areas and their people came into the limelight and drew the attention of the citizens across India, mainly due to speeches delivered by the Prime Minister within and outside the parliament, on the imperative necessity of safeguards for inhabitants of these areas so that their unsophisticated mode of religion, culture, traditions, customs, and art survived.

The Naga rebellion, followed by the demand of the hills for the formation of a separate state, and finally the threat of Chinese incursion into Indian territory, had drawn the attention of everyone toward these scantily known areas.

In the book Philosophy of NEFA, India (Northeast Frontier Agency) by Dr. Varier Elwyn, once a missionary and later the tribal adviser, had put forward in writing the importance of areas in NEFA, its people, and the tribal policy of the government. A foreword by the Prime Minister of India, Pandit Jawaharlal Nehru, supported his views. The book, indeed, was of significant value, more so as it was freely available to the public.

37

THE BOOK ON NEFA, CONFLICTING VIEWS

The book created considerable interest. At table talks in the evenings, where friends, Nagas and Non-Nagas including those from other tribes gathered, invariably the contents of the book and allied subjects came up for discussion. They were educative, enlightening, and interesting. "I have yet to understand why some people are termed tribal," said one of the participants, and lifting the dictionary from a nearby shelf, he read out the meaning given. "Already we have terminology dividing the people of India into linguistic communities and categories like scheduled classes, so why add this additional division of a group called tribal to cause further disintegration?"

"I have tried elucidating an answer from tribal advisers and the author of the book, but even today I am not convinced that it is at all appropriate to use the word. Your doubt appears to be reasonable," said another friend. "It appears to be a legacy of British policy based on the divide and rule policy. Already, we have too many different names for different communities, enough to distinguish ourselves from one another."

"Further, each community is subdivided by religion and class. Even further subdivisions as officers, industrialists, skilled and non-skilled workers, or agriculturists are evident. Divisions are also made due to politics, adding to the confusion. If all the people in the tribal zone dressed alike and spoke the same language, they could be termed as 'tribal', but it is not so. The citizens of Waziristan were also once called tribal, and they have nothing in common with the people of this region.

With all these divisions, which were formed for economic and tribal gains, how can we achieve the emotional and national integration?"

He lit a cigarette and then continued, "We were never as united as during the period when the British quit India, and Sardar Vallabhai Patel was with us, and it is unlikely that we will ever achieve that unity again. The linguistic States and the adoption of Hindi as a national language by legislation have set the basis of unity on fire, which the mighty Pandit Jawaharlal Nehru, to whom India and her progress have become life and blood, is unable to extinguish." "I understand," said a newly appointed officer, "it was the desire of Mahatma Gandhi that states be organized on a linguistic basis and Hindi be made the national language, and his disciple made a promise that it would be fulfilled."

"It may be the case," said the previous speaker, "but one must override decisions arising from sentimental considerations and emotional moments and forget the promises made to the dead, given the changed circumstances and the people's attitude." "One must view many things stone-heartedly. The linguistic states have their advantages, but if Mahatma Gandhi were alive to see the degeneration caused by the process adopted, and the resultant atmosphere torpedoing the unity, he would have himself cried for a halt! If he were alive, we would never have had the fortune to see Pandit Jawaharlal Nehru rising to international fame by the process of his initiative and free thinking. He would have still sat at the feet of Mahatma Gandhi for advice, guidance, and solace."

"English was the medium of official correspondence brought into practice by usages of service, and not by legislation. No one agitated against it; there is no instance where the local dialect suffered annihilation during the British regime. On the contrary, everyone had full freedom to select the medium of instruction and study the languages one wished. A few writers of the caliber of Gurudev Rabindranath Tagore, and eminent writers from other languages, have come into prominence even after the formation of the linguistic states."

"Then why have these linguistic states got different languages for official correspondence and medium of instruction?" queried one of the friends. "Primarily it is an economical move, coupled with political agitation," replied the first speaker. "The motive is to reserve all jobs in services within the state for the residents of the state, who can speak the languages." "As a result, an individual from another state, however efficient maybe, is treated and conspired against, with the view to oust him and make way for a local man. This creates fear in the minds of minorities having different languages within a state and consequent repercussions."

"We do not have to go far away to see the chaos caused. In Assam, there are Assamese, Bengalis, citizens of the hills, Muslims, and a significant percentage of laborers from other states. They wish to be acquainted with their native language and must learn Assamese. Hindi is compulsory and English, even today, is important to keep a link with the outside world. Added to it are the multiple languages among the tribal; tomorrow this phenomenon may encourage different groups of the community, termed as tribal, to seek a separate existence and thus give rebirth to feudalism." "No, it will never occur as long as the word 'tribal' is used to distinguish us from the people of the rest of India and accord us necessary safeguards and sympathetic treatment," said the newly appointed Naga officer, taking out the book "Philosophy of NEFA" from his attaché case. He continued, "you will find in here that what I say is true."

"Put the book away," roared one of the elderly friends who was known for his intellectual brilliance, studious nature, and balanced reviews. Until now, he had listened to passionate discussions, seated in a corner without participating in the discussions. Leaving his chair, he came forward to occupy a vacant one and said, "I do not mean any disrespect either to the learned author or to the Prime Minister who wrote the foreword. The principles outlined in the book are worth studying from the humanitarian point of view, but there ends the importance of the book as I perceive it. I agree that the author of the book has taken pains to study the people and works of other authors on the subject and has quoted extensively to augment his line of thought! Unfortunately, I am neither inclined to agree with all that he has said, nor can I reconcile myself to the fact that it is the right philosophy to be adopted or followed. On the contrary, the book is antagonistic to the integration of India and likely to infuse a spirit of dissension, discord, and anarchy."

His words caused a temporary bewilderment among some listeners, but at the same time infuriated a few admirers of the book. Controlling his excitement, one of them said, "I hope you are not ill today to criticize the author who has even been supported by the Prime Minister, Mr. Nehru." The earlier speaker rose from his seat with laughter and replied after lighting his cigarette, "I am not physically ill, but mentally I am to see the book being produced and its contents being quoted every time in support of anything, as if it were a Bible. Further, I do not have that blind, pathetic faith in Pandit Jawaharlal Nehru to passionately believe that he sees no ill, he speaks no ill, he hears no ill, he cannot err, and all that he says and does is nothing but the unquestionable truth and 100% correct. I have an unprejudiced educated mind and patience enough to reason dispassionately the ideals of our Prime Minister; his views in respect of tribals are indeed admirable, but translated and interpreted wrongly."

"The basic principles on which I not only differ but would recommend confiscation of such books is that it has been based on preconceived ideas inherited from the old regime that the citizens of this tribal hilly area are different from the rest of the people in India and as such they require a special set of officers to govern a special type of administration and special consideration. If the book had been written after careful investigation and study as to what is common between them and other citizens of the advanced part of India, how emotions and integration can be carried out, and what are the best means to preserve their culture, religion, traditions, customs, and art where one could meet the other, probably the book would have taken a different form and theme retaining the principles and ideals cherished by Nehru."

38

THE DEBATES CONTINUE

He looked at the clock. "It is getting late for dinner. Think it over. If necessary, we will discuss it further the next time we meet." Wishing everyone goodbye, he left as suddenly as he had taken part in the discussion.

On a few occasions thereafter, we missed the presence of our friend as he was out on a tour. Not only were some of his friends eager to confront him and make him prove what he had said earlier, but others were anxious to hear him elucidate further. He did join the informal gathering in the evening, right on the day he returned. As he walked in scrutinizing each one of us sitting there and said, "I presume you all must be waiting to cut me to pieces."

"No," replied a Naga friend humorously, "Naga Hills is not yet short of beef or mutton to resort to human flesh, and we are not inclined to feast on your flesh and bones. Let your body be preserved for an honorable burial, and at a mature age in a good place. Anyway, we are eager to hear you enlighten us further on what you have said the other day."

"Certainly! I never speak unless I am clear and convinced about it. I do not expect others to concur with what I say, so criticism is welcome as it may educate me," he paused to light a cigarette and continued, "Let us first consider the ties still existing between the different linguistic states in India, which seem to be at war with each other and more so with the center for economic and political gains. The redeeming factor, which is primarily keeping us all united, for the time being, is the international personality and magical spell of Pandit Jawaharlal Nehru, the disciple of Mahatma Gandhi; next are the political parties, and last but not least are the All-India Services. I see no other potent factor, which comes up to the expectations."

Uninterrupted, he continued. "No other leader in India comes within miles of Pandit Jawaharlal Nehru in being respected, outside and within India, by any standard. Everyone will invariably pray that he lives long to see India become rich economically and politically, but the question that confronts everyone is who is next after Jawaharlal. There are many aspirants, and some may succeed in climbing up the ladder of expectations if they devote their life and blood to the cause of India's progress."

"Whatever it may be, none would be able to manage as well as he does. His personality has made an indelible impression and has a hold over the minds of most citizens, to sway and excite their emotions and sentiments. The successor will be the one who enjoys a similar popularity or one who can hold them together with the support of the armed forces." He paused; none said anything! He continued, "The most important political organization, the Congress, has very few real patriots with firm ideology, the majority being opportunistic, who can rock and roll for personal gain. The communists have a firm ideology, but at least none of us wish to look to Moscow or Peking (Beijing) for guidance and salvation."

"Meanwhile, if anyone, perhaps they may not maintain the ties, but strengthen the solidarity, are the members of the All-India Services. The importance of this service has been visualized in this context, and hence an effort is being made to widen the scope to make it applicable to other departments, plus the recruitments which have been made by the state."

"The party in power may be replaced by the verdict of the people, ministers may come and go, and the ideology and policies of the government may undergo revolutionary change, but the services which form the foundation of the state will remain. But was there a necessity to start a new cadre, called the Indian Frontiers Administrative Service, exclusively for the NEFA and tribal areas? Was it because the personnel of the Indian Administrative Service had no potential to administer tribal areas? Are there no equally backward people in other parts of India who live amidst advanced citizens, retaining their individuality and environment efficiently? How are these people administered by the personnel of the existing services?"

"Do you attribute the discord to the creation of the IFAS cadre?" an officer of the IFAS cadre asked and continued, "The book adequately justifies the creation of it."

"Not exactly," was the reply. "If the philosophy had been formulated early and the cadre based on it to make it effective, I would understand the possible utility and righteousness of it, but it is vice versa; the book is an afterthought. Anyone can appreciate and visualize the importance and necessity of efficient officers of integrity and character to administer the frontier belt and those who could be found in the existing cadres. Further, it is doubtful whether any of the members of the IAS are better than those of other services. On the contrary, without any reflection on the cadre, I will not hesitate to pronounce that at least a portion of them lack character and integrity and have been at one time or another advocates, advisers, and agitators to the cause of discord, dissension, and feudalism."

"Some of you present here have enlightened me about a few members of the IAS who were discrediting the members of other services in public to prove their worth and superiority, instead of establishing it by merit. It is a cowardly tendency to cause trouble! Will it not instill a hatred for other services and initiate a separatist tendency among the tribal by making them believe that they are different from the people of the rest of India and hence need a special separate cadre of officers? Is it a holy sign?"

"Instead of planting seedlings of emotional and national integration, seeds of discord and dissension were sown, resulting in a wish for a separate existence. These are being administered, maybe unwillingly and unknowingly, due to personal egoism, seeking promotion, and playing games. I wonder whether it is by the ideals of the Prime Minister." His words had a mixed reaction among the friends who had gathered there.

One of them, feeling offended, said, "If there was any soundness in your reasoning, do you not feel that the Prime Minister would have noticed the defects earlier and not only disbanded the cadre, but reviewed the whole policy?

"Please do not feel offended over what I put forward. If anyone convinces me that I am wrong, I have a flexible mind with no rigid way of thinking to accept it and mend my views accordingly. But this is not the case with politicians and political parties. They will never accept, in consideration of the popular esteem of the party and its leaders, that they have erred or committed a blunder and revise with humility any decision taken by them. They invariably make a scapegoat of the people, government servants, laying blame on them for the failures to save their own skin and popularity."

He said this with a smile and narrated a story of a single parent! "Our Prime Minister's case is like a single parent, with lofty ideals and ambitions. However, deeply engrossed in his preoccupations outside, the care of his children, whom he loves, is passed on. He also cherishes a smooth-running house with all comforts and a pleasing atmosphere, undisturbed. Besieged with files and visitors at his home, he has no time to go into details or be bothered about it. In such an eventuality, he has no alternative but to trust and believe the caretaker in all good faith. He lets the children grow and the house run under the caretaker's guidance! If the caretaker takes precautions to inform him that all is well, giving reports to suit his ideas. Even if his children complain, being engrossed in other things, he discards the complaints as childish talk even though it may hurt and displease the children for he has the word of the caretaker that it is not so, and everything is sailing smoothly."

Lighting a cigarette, he continued, "When a new state for Nagas was formed, people of Tuensang district, who are also Nagas, agitated to save their garden from exploitation by their brothers from the districts of Kohima and Mokokchung. In Assam, where the chieftainship and unquestionable loyalty toward it existed not so long ago, due to divergence of language, dress, customs, and traditions between each district, their demand for a separate state is acceded to. God forbid the same chaos the seizing different tribes of NEFA, who have so far harmoniously stayed as good neighbors and leading them once again to the age of violence or violent feudalism."

He paused, poured water into a glass, and sipping it said, "During my recent tour, I heard a great deal about the safeguard of essentials for the tribal, irrespective of their location, whether here in the Naga Hills, Assam, or Nepal. I cannot perceive why there is this cry. I understand that since it has been emphasized in the book 'Philosophy of NEFA' with the foreword by the Prime Minister, it has assumed the greatest significance. India has been invaded repeatedly, and invaders remained for years. There was even a period when systematic destruction of Hindu shrines happened. But despite the impact of foreign powers and their faiths lasting over centuries, the culture, religion, traditions, customs, languages, and art of most of the people in India have not only survived but remained intact."

"Even when literacy was limited to only a few, the advances made by our civilization did impact our diverse cultures naturally and for the good of the people. The tendency to seek what is good in others and adopt if suitable to one's environment and for their betterment is inevitable! But despite these changes and the foreign domination, the Bengalis have retained their "dhoti and saree," Assamese their "mekhela and chadar," Rajasthan their "Ghagra," the Maharashtrian their "folk dances and Lazim," the South Indians their "Kathakali." In those days, the foreign rulers had no communal and tribal advisers to render advice on how to retain the culture and the individual arts and religion of the citizens of our land. Now when we are the rulers of our land, we want to create divisions on the pretext of safeguards to let them live in their way. It is nothing but a bogey and creation of vested interests."

"Today, the fear that the rest of India will invade the tribal belt by using force does not exist. Foreign capital and experts in collaborations are inevitable in an underdeveloped area. It is being done in India. Then why deny its benefit to the tribal belt on the plea of safeguarding their culture? The doors to these tribal belts are very close to the people of the rest of India."

"I will try to convince you subsequently. But the real danger which will wipe out the Earth below the feet of the citizens of the tribal belt, is from another direction. I feel that people concerned are not aware of it, or it is being ignored as inevitable." He rose from the chair and, taking his headgear, said, "I must go. It is already late, and the discussion is at your disposal to continue or to stop it here."

He was not inclined, on his initiative, to speak when we met next. He occupied his usual seat in the rear, but everyone pressed him to clarify the suspense created by his words. "The principles outlined in the preface by the Prime Minister, I feel, have been stretched too far in the book. The main one is the emphasis on administrators attiring themselves like people under their jurisdiction, to make the former feel one and nearer to the latter and help them to retain their style in their dress. A sheep covering itself in tiger skin will not be able to hoodwink even the animals. In the former case, the sheep is bound to fall prey to the hunger of the tiger; the tiger will inevitably cause a scare in the herd of sheep."

"A tribal appreciates the honesty of a spade being called a spade, the process advocated is a primitive way of thinking. It is like trying to deceive Lord Buddha to draw his blessings. As has been rightly brought out in the book, clothes worn originate from personal convenience, which is also important. Even the primitive people of Nepal and most orthodox Lamas, including the Dalai Lama, have discarded their traditional headgear in favor of an evening felt hat and the Gurkha hat as worn by the armed forces. Even though it appears out of place with their traditional attire, it is convenient in the sense that it is liked and available, and it gives protection from heat and cold. Given hygienic considerations, whether the clothes worn by the people of hilly regions should change or not is better left to the scientists, doctors, and psychologists."

"The same considerations applied to nudity; if people have sufficient money for clothing and if it is available, they would certainly like to attire themselves in a dignified fashion. Feeling ashamed is the result of an inferiority complex, shortcomings, and a feeling that one is out of place. If an individual is convinced regarding the righteousness of his actions, he would not hesitate to act."

"Discourse in the book regarding the types of religions people may adopt in the future appears to be unexplainable. Why this question? Do the people of the tribal belt have no religious faith? Unable to reason and subsequently express clearly, they are not able to explain the origin and its concept. Their religion has primitive virtues of being connected to the land, body, and soul. If it has served the purpose to preserve their faith in the supernatural being, it is good enough."

"Unfortunately, the citizens of these hilly regions of Nepal, Assam, and Nagaland hills had no script of their own. As such, messages of the almighty and their benevolence are passed on to the following generations verbally by the aged, and it will be the same for all future generations. With the inherent defect of verbal messages, the words may have changed, but the principles remain the same."

"It could have been the case with other religions too. It was not Ram, Krishna, Buddha, Paigambar, Guru Nanak, and Christ who authored the holy books. Engrossed in the upliftment of humanity, they had no time to hold a pen. It was disciples who took to writing, and in a way that could be understood by all. No one can say that it was motivated by a desire to spread their master's message to every corner of the Earth. The books, which were written by the disciples, did try to make it more colorful and appealing!"

"Foreign Christian missionaries were the first literate outsiders to have the privilege to enter these areas and establish unrestricted contact with the citizens. In the recent past, the work of the missionaries for the humanitarian cause and upliftment in the field of education is undisputedly praiseworthy. They adopted the Roman script for their language and wrote textbooks to educate their students in their script. Also, being motivated by a desire to spread their faith and convert people to it or being unable to grasp the basis and concept of the religious faith of the locals, due to lack of exposure to holy books other than their own, they ignored it. In the absence of any institution and organization and being unable to educate its inhabitants on their faiths, they were easily converted to Christianity."

He continued, "A careful study and scrutiny of the concept of faith, as it existed among the inhabitants of the hilly regions, will indicate their faith in Shiva and Shakti. Even today they worship these 2 deities in some imaginary form, but the words have lost the original pronunciation due to the defect of being passed on verbally over generations."

"The temples of Shiva at Guwahati and near the foothills were initiated, built by the people of the hills as places of worship, but the temples have been taken over by the more educated and learned, like the priests from the plains! As Maharashtrians performing as the chief priests at Badrinath in Garhwal hills and Pashupatinath in Nepal."

"It indicates that hillmen were once equally advanced in the creative art of constructing temples for worship, and later they made way for the learned. However, the safeguards and restrictions on entry of others than the residents deprived them of the benefit of furthering their design and retaining contact with the like-minded. It also moved them to seclusion and a primitive livelihood, bringing about the decline and the disappearance of the religiously learned among them, to withstand slaughter from other faiths. If it were not so, Christianity would have found equal scope in other hilly regions of India like those hills of Assam and the surrounding area."

He lit a cigarette and continued, "The thoughts expressed in the book suggest a likely disinclination of the residents of Nepal toward Hinduism, as eating beef is forbidden in Hindu mythology and a cow is worshipped. However, there is also a partial attitude and soft corner for Christianity, seen as a probable substitute for existing religions. These attitudes are probably the outcome of deep roots and favor toward it, due to a long association in the subconscious mind of the author."

He paused and asked, "Any questions?" "Go ahead," a young officer said. "Even if it is presumed that India is a Hindu domain, religious intolerance in India has been rare; if not, other faiths would not have found a foothold on the Indian soil."

"On the contrary, accommodativeness and appreciation of art, culture, costumes of invaders, and different religious faiths have been encouraging, even exemplary! Even though Shivaji assumed the title of "God Brahma Pratiksha," tolerance, appreciation, and recognition of other faiths, their saints, and shrines were noteworthy, resulting in even the Pathans enlisting in his army, which helped Shivaji to establish Dharmaraj (rules of righteousness), Hindu worship of Ashva, Nagaraj (cobra), Raksha (tree), Agni (fire), Jala Devata (deity of water), and so forth."

"It does not mean that Hindus will decline to ride a horse, cut a tree for fuel, harness the river, fail to kill a cobra, or hesitate to extinguish a fire in a house. Despite Hindu respect for a cow, because it parts with milk like a mother, helping to build up a healthy body and mind, thousands of cows are slaughtered on the very Indian soil, as food for those of other faiths. Perhaps restrictions on cow slaughter and worship of water, cobra, fire, etc., originated to restrict human beings in the early days. A revered approach to a snake to keep it from being harmed unnecessarily, not to cut trees indiscriminately but to care for them as they give shade and fuel and so on."

"To create a scare in Naga Hills, that the Hindus may not accept them as one with them, because Nagas eat beef, is a wicked and an imprudent move. For ages, people of the frontier hilly regions had contact with Buddhist culture from the north and Hindu culture in the South until safeguards put an Iron Curtain over the area, banning entry from the South. Even today, one knows truly little about what transpires within the inner line, except through official spokespersons and communication. While the people of Nepal could live harmoniously with Tibetans and allow them to construct Buddhist monasteries on their soil, why be afraid of Hinduism, which is akin to Buddhism?"

"Even if, after contact with Buddhism, most of them refrained from embracing it as a faith and retained their religious culture, traditions, customs, and costumes, why be afraid of Hindus? To initiate such thoughts, to make them perceive such an eventuality, is the result of a prejudiced mind. There is no precedent to show that protagonists of Hinduism and Buddhism undertake any organized conversion, though intake of any voluntary submission is not declined. It is also worth considering whether the citizens of NEFA found spiritual solace and inspiration from the ancient faith they had. If it was not so, they would have discarded it much earlier and chosen either Buddhism or Hinduism, which surrounds it from all sides. If this did not happen, it is evident that their religion was adequate. References to these areas in Ramayana and Mahabharata indicate that Hindu culture has traversed these areas without affecting the faith, traditions, customs, and costumes of the residents."

He lit another cigarette, the 10th in the chain, and continued, "Whenever there is talk regarding people of Nepal and other residents of hills in this area, there is an emphasis on differences and not what is common. Are we trying to find out how one community can differ from another, retained by safeguards in similar regulations, or are we trying to find out what is common between us, exploit it, and base everlasting unity on it?"

"Though I did not have time as some other fortunate ones have, to travel to every remote corner of this region, from my experience, I see so much in the common worth application, between inhabitants of hilly regions, citizens of Assam, and inhabitants of the rest of India."

"If you take a Khasi, in ancient dress, a dhoti and turban, and the locals of Konkan in Maharashtra, Indian experts will not be able to distinguish one from another unless they speak. The details of ancient wedding procedures concur more than they differ with myths and superstitions and have more similarities than dissimilarities in ancient dress, art, customs, traditions, and costumes. Similarities outscore differences.

Changes will be there with the vastness of the land, climate, difficult lines of communication, availability of commodities and heritage."

"Even within the Angami area of Naga Hills, those in the north differ from the southerners and westerners, even though they are within 2 hours of walking distance. In address, accent, haircut, time, mode of religious functions, and a clamor for recognition, Chakesanges differ from Angami in every respect and there are many such differences within Nagas!"

Turning to his host, the speaker asked, "I think I have steamed off enough for now. Should we stop for the day?" Before the host could reply, another friend shouted, "No! Not even if it is dawn. The other day, you talked about danger from an unknown corner and placed us in suspense. Out with it, we do not wish to have more sleepless nights guessing about it. You can have your drink if you do not wish to miss it," and requested the host to get drinks!

The speaker pleaded repeatedly for the others not to press him to speak on the subject, as his views might not be appreciated by them, other friends elsewhere, and by the ideologists in power. However, his request proved futile, as everyone forced him to narrate his views, determined to even wait until dawn to hear him.

39

THE REAL DANGERS ARE FROM UNEXPECTED PLACES!

After an informal, irrelevant chat over a glass of wine, he began to speak in earnest!

"To put it methodologically, I would say the danger arises from the following:

First: Using the word tribal. We have already discussed the impropriety of using the word tribal. While every effort is made to eradicate communal and linguistic divisions, why add 'tribalism'? If indeed the differences are to be continued, remember that the components of the tribal belt in question differ from each other. However, only the differences from other communities of India are being capitalized."

"Will it not be worth restraining this false sense of unity and preparing the ground for more discussions? Try to reorient the basis of existence and coexistence, understand the role of religion and how it is the common basis of culture and traditions. On it depends the outlook and all the subsidiary points in the daily walk of life!

"Second: Absence of institutes, organizations, and funds to protect the originally existing religious faith of citizens of these areas. There is an unquestionable necessity as the people have found solace and spiritual inspiration in their faiths so far. It cannot be denied that a certain vagueness exists regarding parts of the faith and hence it is difficult to make it sound and concrete."

"Third: There is a need for research and study by learned persons who are disinterested in the expansion of any other religion, who can dispassionately reason and formulate their special individual faith and reduce it in writing in their dialect."

Attitudes and inclinations of the members of the IFS cadre. Today we see an intricate machinery of advisers and experts from the special cadre to protect the art, culture, traditions, customs, and costumes of the citizens of Nepal and other hills. Will it last long or will you succeed in retaining it, if the basis of the religious faith changes for lack of money?"

"Fourth: Advance of religion other than their original one and the resultant change in outlook. The fact is that missions, especially the Christian missions, are very well organized. They have devoted their lives to an ambition to convert every person on Earth. In addition, these missions are financially sounder than many nations, financed from within and outside."

"Nothing more need be said about the existence and utility of the IFAS. The intention behind it was undoubtedly sound, but the outlook of the incumbents requires reorientation if it is to fulfill the task allotted to it under existing regulations. Entry of any individual or organizational workers, political or religious, close to the NEFA is restricted. However, the Christian mission will gain a foothold on the soil despite the restriction and vigilance, and before any other mission is established to protect the existing faith."

"How could it materialize? Do the Christian missions have 'wings' and which are invisible?" asks a friend.

"No, but they have invisible motivated supporters. Interested individuals have prepared the ground for it. Christian missions send children for education to mission schools beyond the inner line where they are converted. Once they return to the land as full-fledged Christians, no one can deny the sons of the soil, constructing churches for worship and alluring others. Establishment of mission centers under local experts will be the next step, even if the inner line regulations granting safeguards and preventing exploitation continue to be operative."

"I am not an antagonist of the Christian faith, but given all the good and bad said and heard of the government policy for tribals based on the idea of our Prime Minister, it is worth considering whether, in the light of the impact of Christianity on the people of the hilly region other than NEFA, the purpose of safeguards is fulfilled."

"A careful study will show that in the educational and medical fields, the mission has rendered unparalleled humanitarian service, but wiped out the religious faith inherited by the citizens from their ancestors. People were lured by the concrete form of Christianity as compared to the verbal and vague form of their faith and practice hitherto, and in the absence of any organization to retain and protect it and holy books to enlighten the hearts adhering to the faith. When no one is allowed entry into these areas, why the Christian missions under foreigners have a lot of footholds, is better left to dispassionate reasoning by wise men."

"The methods adopted for change, which would not free from coercion, curbs, and rules, enforced for converts varied in different areas in United Jaintia and Khasi hills. The locals' workers were encouraged to drink distilled homemade brew, driving men to potency, and increasing the characteristics of easy virtue among a different sex. On the contrary, in Naga hills, converts were prohibited from consuming wine in any form, not that all those who embrace Christianity abide by it."

"Has Christianity not uprooted the age-long deep roots of culture, traditions, customs, and art of the people? With the change of faith, culture and other allied subjects automatically undergo transformation. One will find considerable change in customs, religion, and culture and decay of traditions everywhere in Naga Hills, Lucia Hills (Mizoram), united Jaintia and Khasi Hills, Garo Hills, and the 2 hilly subdivisions of Manipur where foreign missionaries had sway. Much of what was original, including the tunes, which have undergone transformations by making a cry for safeguards a boogie. What the invaders for centuries could not achieve in other parts of India has been instilled in the minds of people in these hilly regions by the missions. The worst of it is the Anglo-tribal outlook created in their minds, driving the Christian converts of the area distance apart in culture and political outlook from the rest of the people of India. The results of such an attitude need no elucidation, as it is emphatically enumerated in the book 'Bhawani Junction.'"

"Those hills, man, of this region who are Christians, scorn everything of Indian origin, including the national dress, but address people from the rest of India as Indians and aliens. Separate "Khels" have been established in mostly villages in Naga Hills by those who have adopted Christianity as their religion. This is the very basis of the separatist tendency, which is inherited from the sermons, with emphasis on the slogan: only those who believe in Christianity will receive salvation when the world ends, which is not far off, while others will not. I spent many days with Christian ministries and attended sermons in church elsewhere, but never heard of such a cry and compromising diligence."

"A few Naga ministers like Reverend Kizungliba Ao are an exception to it, advocating tolerance and appreciation of other religions. Yet they are but a drop in this ocean of hatred and pro-Western influence. This unaccommodating and separatist attitude, instilled by the foreign missionaries, has been the cause of political upheaval in this region. Without hesitation, no one can say that the brains behind the independent movement in Naga hills and the separate hills state in Assam are the Christians: 'the non-Christians kept aloof.'"

"I fully agree with you," said an officer born and brought up in these hills, who would not embrace Christianity. "What you indicated is the hidden truth. I wonder how you grasped it. I have tried to discuss it with my superiors, but I was rewarded with scorn. They said that experts and advisers on tribal affairs do not agree with the concept and, being experts, know much better than myself, son of the soil." Then pointing toward his friend and himself, he said, "I feel so happy that besides we 2, another officer thinks likewise. My talk with these experts on tribal affairs at all levels was also discarded as trifling."

"I am happy," said the speaker, "someone concurs with me. So far, I was a solitary individual, to think in that direction. You can further imagine the hills of this separatist tendency from the fact that over so many years the Ramkrishna mission has failed to get adequate space to build a college at Shillong, while Christian missionaries can get land as and when they require. The Christian mission hospitals accord free medical treatment to poor and needy healthy men of the Christian faith but not to others. Anyway, I must end this stuff so that I can avail of the opportunity to have supper, even though it must be cold."

"Lastly, the Fifth: Outlook of the advisers and experts on tribal affairs. Among the expert advisers on tribal affairs, not a single son of the soil or a Hillsman from these areas is seen. Probably most of the advisers have lived with the tribals only in imagination. It is a different thing to know all about fruit from a book than to taste it."

An Indian scholar, given an opportunity, facilities, and means of livelihood, surely would have provided a more realistic theme and views. If a learned person like our doctor Radhakrishnan had authored this book, undoubtedly the philosophy outlined would have been worth adopting!"

"Earlier, I had mentioned that the attitude of all the government servants is similar and the advisers and experts on tribal affairs are not an exception to it. They prosper individually by devising concepts to fit in with the ideals of the master."

"Probably you are too hard on them for anyway it would have been better if you had gone into detail," one of them said. "Truth is not palatable to any and detail exposes it to an extent of bitterness. I may do so when I retire, and if my family members feel content to live within the means of my retirement pension. At present, I am busy if not overworked, with matters of another nature which depend on my daily income of bread and butter and even progress and promotion.

"Some of us, after due thought, may like to talk over the subject matter and issue a rejoinder," said the listener with a pat on his back. Most welcome. Unless there are rejoinders and criticisms, one can never reach perfection. Further, I do not hold a monopoly on being correct. I returned home recapitulating the lecture I had heard on "poetry and war."

40

IT WAS TIME FOR ME TO MOVE ON, WITH INDELIBLE MEMORIES

On 15th August 1958, I made up my mind to request the authorities to relieve me from my posting in Naga Hills. I signed the letter 2 days later on my birthday. It was the time the Naga hostiles had warned that any vehicle flying the Indian national flag and plying on the road would be fired upon, and the occupants killed.

I had an invitation from a battalion of the Maratha Light Infantry for the flag hoisting ceremony, children's rally, and lunch at Jakhama village. Very keen to go to Jakhama, as the villagers, the elders, and the officers of the units were my friends. As soon as the flag hoisting at Kohima was over, I returned and instructed the driver to fill the tank of the vehicle and also fix a pole and tie a large flag on the pole. I then told Surendra Mohan Kar I was going to Mao, a village which is on the boundary of the Naga Hills and Manipur state, and that I would attend the function at Jakhama on the way back.

Very perturbed on hearing my plans, he pleaded that I should not go as no vehicle was seen plying on the road. It was a holiday, and he reminded me of the dinner we had arranged for the occasion. Assuring him that I would return before the invitees turned up, I dismissed the driver and drove the jeep myself with the flag flying, which could be seen from a great distance.

Then I saw Visar Angami and John Angami, who were also keen to go to Jakhama to participate in the function. I stopped to give them a ride. John gave Visar Angami a friendly dig, saying, "You can shield all of us if anyone fires at us." "Let them fire," Visar said and added that he had heard such threats too often and claimed that even if a bullet pierced his skin, only pure Madhu would flow out, not even a drop of blood, making all of us roar with laughter!

Deliberately slow, I drove to Mao, stopped at each village en route, and met the villagers on the road. It was with immense pride that we saw the national flag flying at each village, and the men, women, and children proceeding to the place of the rally. Behind the national flag carried by the older children, it was a wonderful feeling. Children greeted us with "Jai Hind." After a visit to Moa and Khuzama village where Independence Day celebrations were in full swing, we returned to Jakhama, the village of Visar Angami, to participate in their children's rally and lunch. Despite a drizzle, everyone participated with full vigor. The function at Jakhama was symbolic of the people's will and desire to live in peace. After all the participants dispersed, we started our journey back to Kohima. At the last moment, many items were arranged for the people as they had expressed a desire to take part in the sports. Visar and John were to participate in the football match to be played at Kohima, between gentlemen and services, the former as a player and the latter as a spectator-cum-linesman.

Visar was eager to return to Kohima despite the Madhu and rum he had consumed. He looked at the rain on the ground and laughingly said, "The ground at Kohima will be muddier; it will be great playing in on the muddy field. Not only will it take tons of energy to move the ball through the mud, but I can throw some of it on the selective spectators who will entertain themselves, seeing us covered with mud." Visar sat on the bonnet of the vehicle throughout the journey, singing songs aloud with the rum bottle in his hand and holding on to the pole of the national flag for support. En route, passengers joined him in singing. The football match was played, and as the ball would not move in the mud, each side was eager to score. Halfway, Visar turned it into a rugby game.

Before I parted company with my friends and the Naga Hills, members of my family joined me during the winter vacation. Everyone, all my friends, asked the same question repeatedly, "When will you come again? Do come, we will miss you a lot." I could not give a reply as I knew not what was in store for me in the future. In the nearby room, my daughter was humming the song "K Sara Sara."

The parting was very touching. All the familiar faces there, who came to bid me farewell, none could speak, being choked with emotion. My daughter Kshiteeja, who rarely becomes emotional, burst into tears. When she stopped crying, she said, "Daddy, how sad to part with friends who loved you so much. Probably, you will never return to these beautiful hills."

She was right, strange thoughts crept up into my mind as I drove to Dimapur. That from tomorrow I would be a memory among my friends here in the Naga Hills, a thing of the past. I had contemplated building a memorial to all my staff killed in the Navy hills. It had remained to be completed. Would it ever be built? This chain of thoughts continued. I told myself to forget the past and look to the future. My annual leave gave me a most welcome change as I moved about from place to place visiting my relatives and friends. In Bombay, I saw a Marathi drama entitled Duritanche Timiri Javo staged by renowned artists of Maharashtra. The theme was about a pious and learned person who was declared mad and laughed at during his lifetime. Finally, he was stoned to death for his attempt to take people nearer to spiritualism because his utterings were above the understanding of the common people.

The play depicted that among the present-day society striving for material gain, there is a common pattern where very often, the true ministers of God and true unappreciated social workers, who sacrificed everything for the good of the people, were shamed as mad and insane. Such has become our morality that once these godly ones are dead, the hypocritical society remembers all the good for which they stood and erects a memorial to them or even carves stone images of them to be worshipped. How realistic was this drama?!

On the termination of my leave, I was at Shillong, awaiting posting orders when I was informed that the governor had decided to meet me for discussions. It was nothing new, as whenever I came to Shillong from Kohima, Sir Fazal Ali summoned me for a discussion, and it often lasted for many hours. On many occasions, I was especially summoned to Shillong to meet him, but now I had nothing to do with the subject with which we used to discuss.

When I went to meet him, he was lying on the bed with files by his side. In the last 3 years, it was the first time I had seen him attending to work in his bed. With his usual smile of welcome, he made kind inquiries about the welfare of my family and myself before he touched upon the subject. Though he looked tired, his enthusiasm for work was admirable. He opened file after file and discussed them with zeal over 2 hours, saying that he was exhausted. As I sought permission to go, he asked me to sit down, asking if I was tired.

"No, Sir, not me," I replied politely. He asked me to sit if I had no other appointment. Opening another file, he said that these were awaiting his decision for a long time, while the problems in Naga Hills had to be promptly solved. "I feel guilty for the delay, but I was indeed unwell and could not concentrate on work to make important decisions." Then Shrimati Fazal Ali walked in to give him medication for the second time, and when she left, he asked me to pull my chair closer to him and said, "Do you feel disappointed as your work has not been recognized?"

"The disappointment was a temporary phase," I replied. "But it is no longer there. My conscience is clear, and I am happy and contented as I did my best for the people and the nation, and the people loved me. I am happy with the thought and grateful to you, Sir, for asking!"

"I would not have been surprised if you had felt disappointed," said Fazal Ali, holding my hand. "If I were in your position, I would have felt the same way. You are aware of my admiration for your ability and devotion to duty. You also know the efforts made by me to get your work recognized. Your material loss is great. You have suffered financially and in service, as you believed in us. Since you believed in us, you told us the truth so that we would arrive at the right decisions. Despite enormous pressure, you did not deviate from the right path. It is indeed creditable as few servicemen have that courage."

"Truth is not palatable to many of us these days. My words and appreciation did appeal to the leaders higher up, but they are not free in this system of bureaucracy to act on their own; probably someone high up in the service is opposed to you, whatever it may be. Please remember that very rarely true workers are rewarded in full; on the other hand, all those whose services are recognized on Republic Day deserve it too. We are content that you have done your best for the people and the nation. God bless you."

He appeared even more tired. I thanked him and sought his permission to leave. He told me that he would send for me after a few days for further discussion on certain other points, but it never materialized. He passed away a few days later.

AUTHOR BIO

L t. Col. S.S. Pandit was born in Nagpur on 17th August 1911, in Nagpur, which was a part of Central Provinces during British Raj. In the early 1930s, he joined the Indian Army and was posted to the 7th Battalion of the 1st Punjab Regiment stationed at Jhelum city, which currently lies in the Pakistani segment of Punjab. Later, for a significant part of his army career, he belonged to the 5th Regiment of the Gorkha Rifles, which was posted to the Burma Front during the last few years of the IInd World War. Significantly, the Gorkha Regiment, along with many others, played an important role in the famous Battle of Kohima – Imphal, which the British Allied Forces fought and won against the Japanese Army during the period 1943-44. As per the records of the British Army National Museum, the Battle of Kohima was so fierce and decisive that it proved to be a turning point in the II World War on the eastern front and was instrumental in the eventual retreat of the Japanese Army.

After the end of the Second World War, Lt. Col. Pandit's Battalion was posted to Waziristan, Khyber Pakhtoonwa in today's Pakistan. After independence, he was transferred to the Jat Regiment/Gurkha & Garhwal Rifles. Later, the Indian government selected him to head the Northeastern Unit of the Intelligence Bureau in the area known at that time as the Tuensang Frontier division. For a certain period, it was administered by the Northeast Frontier Agency as well and was a part of it.

Lt. Col. Pandit settled down in Pune after his retirement where he established the "Goodwill" Company, which was dedicated to employing ex-army personnel. He died on 2nd May 1983. Although the achievements of the officers from the Intelligence Bureau are not published in the public domain as a convention, one can state in retrospect that Lt. Col. Pandit certainly earned the complete trust and faith of the people and agencies he worked for, be they army soldiers, IB colleagues, bosses of the administrative establishment, or the Naga hostiles and the common folk. That they all reposed faith in him stands as testimony to his commitment to his work and character.

MAP

N
Arunachal Pradesh
ASSAM
Nagaland
Meghalaya
Manipur
Tripura
Mizoram
Inhabited by Nag-Community
0   100   200

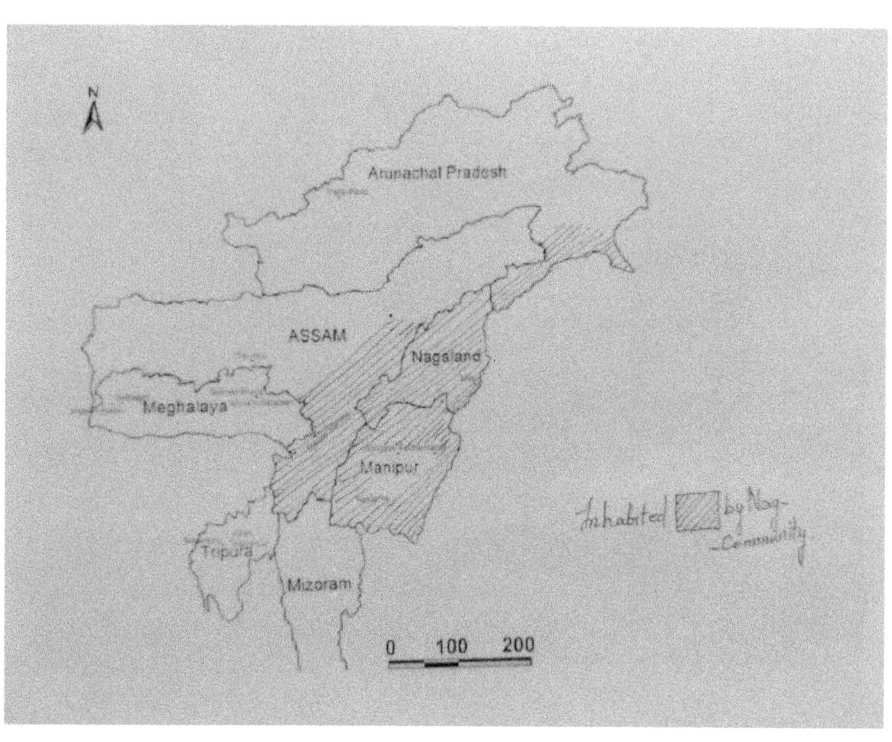